God, Where Are You?

God, Where Are You?

Meditations on the Old Testament

Carlos Mesters

Translated by John Drury

ORBIS BOOKS

Maryknoll, New York 10545

Originally published in 1972 as *Deus, Onde Estas?*
by Editôra Vega, S.A., Belo Horizonte, Brazil

This English translation is based on chapters 1-10 of the original
Portuguese edition

English translation copyright©1977 by Orbis Books

Orbis Books, Maryknoll, New York 10545

Library of Congress Cataloging in Publication Data

Mesters, Carlos.
    God, where are you?

    Translation of Deus, onde estás?
    1.   Bible. O.T.— Criticism, interpretation, etc.
I.   Title.
BS1171.2.M4713   221.6   76-41356
ISBN 0-88344-162-4

"Be always ready with your defense whenever you are called to account for the hope that is in you . . . "

1 PETER 3:15

Contents

Introduction

"God, where are you?" The question is hardly a new one. Many before us have asked it. It is the kind of question that calls for an answer that will have a profound impact on the direction we take in life. Hence there is some value in having someone around who might be able to point us in the right direction as we look for a response.

Among the many responses already given to the question, there is one that is recorded in history and that still continues to make an impression on people today. It is the response of the Bible, which has become a bestseller in over a thousand different languages and which has sold over a billion copies.

1

The Bible is like an old family album containing all sorts of pictures and snapshots. Some record important events: weddings, newborn babies, baptisms, the house newly purchased, and so forth.

Other photos record events of seeming unimportance: a family picnic on the weekend, with no date attached, and so forth. The standards for judging whether a particular photo is important or not are quite relative. A photo of a smiling baby lying naked on a bearskin rug, taken with an old, cheap camera, can be far more important than an expensive family portrait taken by a professional photographer. Both are useless when one registers for working papers; they do not serve that particular purpose. All the pictures are useful for the album, however. It preserves them all, organizing them in its own disordered way according to the rhythms of family life and thus offering us a faithful portrait of the family in question. It is a pleasure for the children and grandchildren to leaf through the pages of the album. They learn who they are and where they came from. Indeed all the photos are important in terms of this purpose, even though they might not seem to be at first glance.

Such is the Bible. It has a little bit of everything: formal official portraits and snapshots of casual moments. Some items were meant to provide explicit documentation; others have no purpose except to draw a smile from the reader. The Bible is the faithful portrait of a people preserved in organized disorder. The children and grandchildren can leaf through its hoary pages to learn who they are and thus fashion an awareness of their own membership in that people.

2

But why is it that this album should be so important for us? Wouldn't the complex and varied history of our own country be enough for us today? In
one sense it certainly does provide us with enough
material. But the point is that many of us at least go
through life with certain questions for which we
cannot find an adequate answer in our family and
national album. Where is God? In what way, if any,
does our national history have anything to do with
God? And if God is somehow present in the midst
of it all, what criteria do we have so that we can
discover God's presence? How are we to determine
and give direction to the course of history that we
are putting together? We all seem to have our own
ideas about the future. Where are we to find some
means of discriminating among them and knowing
that we are relying on something certain insofar as
the future is concerned? These are some of the
serious questions that arise in the minds of people
who really ponder life. The direction we take in life
will depend in no small measure on our answers to
these questions.

The people of the Bible, living in their particular
time and historical situation, raised these same
questions and tried to formulate answers. The direction they took in life was based on the answers
they fashioned. They were on a journey and, to the
wonderment of all, they arrived at their destination:
the resurrection of Christ. The photos preserved in

the Bible deal with this journey, tracing its course from beginning to end.

We Christians believe that the route followed by the people in the Bible is a sure route, the route of God himself. Hence Christians read the Bible and offer it as an indispensable tool for reflection. They see it as a great help in the attempt to analyze reality and find answers for the questions raised by life. They see the history of the people in the Bible as a pattern of action that provides certainty and that is guaranteed by God. Hence they study the Bible, not just to find out what happened in the distant past, but also and primarily to get a better grasp of the sense and purpose of what is happening today in our history. It is this sort of Bible study that is taking on prime importance today, more so than it ever did before.

3

Never in history has the Bible been subjected to such close exegetical and hermeneutical scrutiny as it has been over the past hundred years. Practically every phrase and word of the Bible has been closely analyzed for the sake of its correct meaning. The literature is now so extensive that one feels compelled to specialize in some particular sector of biblical exegesis.

As time went on, however, something seemed to go wrong with this immense panoply of scholarly apparatus. The field of biblical study with its ever growing areas of specialization is like the case of the electronic computer that was not working. There seemed to be some defect that the professional technicians could not pinpoint. They formulated their questions, fed them into the machine, and pressed the button; but nothing happened. The computer would not respond. The defect actually was simple: The computer was not plugged in. It had not occurred to the professionals to check this simple but basic point. They checked every piece of equipment in the computer but could not find anything wrong. Then one morning a janitor cleaning up noticed the problem.

In the field of biblical interpretation, something has not been functioning as it should in the great complex of scholarly machinery. The professionals press the button, but they get no response to the questions life raises. The professionals are trying to pinpoint the defect, and a host of books have appeared to show people "how to read and interpret the Bible." Again the defect is simple and serious: Biblical interpretation is not plugged into real life. It is almost wholly preoccupied with the past, with telling us exactly what took place back then. It does not tell us anything about the meaning and purpose of what is happening here and now. It reminds us of a person who is presented with a microscope and spends a whole lifetime examining how the microscope is put together, without ever studying anything under it.

If it were simply a matter of learning what happened in the past, we would have no need of the Bible. Many things happened in the past of which there is no trace at all in the Bible. Our interest in preserving all that happened to the people of the Bible hinges on the belief that these people and their experiences have something to tell us about our lives today. This would seem to be the proper and principal reason for reading and interpreting the Bible: so that we may cull the message it contains, and thus be aided in answering the questions posed to us by life.

4

As in the case of the electronic computer, it was not the professional experts who first noticed the defect in biblical interpretation. It was simple people trying to sweep up the corridors of life. From the wisdom they had acquired through living, they posed certain questions of their own, and thus made it clear that it made little sense to restrict biblical interpretation and exegesis to the study of the past. They put a simple but serious question to exegesis: "What does all this have to do with our lives today?" And thus they managed to plug the apparatus of scholarship back into the wall socket, once again connecting exegesis with the current of real life.

Hence our main concern in this book will not be to elucidate what happened in the past. Instead, by studying past happenings we shall try to find an answer to questions that we raise about life here and now. We shall try to restore to the word of God the function that it ought to have, which is to serve as a light on the pathway of life, as a help to our own reflective analysis of present-day reality in all its complexity. Then the word can help to insure life's movement toward the resurrection in which we believe and whose power is already operative in those who do believe (see Eph 1:19–23).

5

Today, however, we are faced with a lack of communication. There is a short-circuit between us and the Bible. We do not understand each other. The Bible speaks, but its words are foreign to us. Where does the fault lie: in us or in the Bible? When two people can no longer understand each other, one tends to place the blame on the other. We tend to do the same with the Bible. In biblical interpretation we start from the premise that the cause of the difficulties lies in the Bible, not in ourselves. Our ignorance and our inability to understand the Bible are apparently due to the fact that it is such a difficult book. Hence any introduction to the study of the Bible should clarify the difficulties the Bible contains and thus re-establish the communication that has been interrupted.

My point of view in this book is quite the opposite. The principal problem is not the Bible but in ourselves, in the way we approach the Bible. My aim will not be to clarify the difficulties in the Bible for the reader. There are many good books around that tackle that task. My aim here is to correct the flaw in our own sight; to change the tint of the glasses with which we read the Bible; to show that the alleged beam in the Bible—that is, the difficulties it contains—is really nothing more than a speck of dust (see Mt 7:3).

6

I entered the world of the Bible through a gateway that was opened through long years of study. Living with other people, however, has taught me that there is another gateway into the Bible, which is in fact a much older one, that was used quite often by the Fathers of the Church. Today, however, it is often locked up or even completely forgotten. Yet it enables us to discover quite directly what the Bible is trying to say to us. I should like to provide the key to this gateway in the pages of this book.

Many generations of Christians passed through the gateway in question. It was well-worn with constant use. But it was new to me, giving new value to what I had studied and placing it all in a new light. I do not mean to suggest that my studies were a waste of time; they were not. My studies were very worthwhile in fact. The only problem was that they shed very little light on the corridors of here-and-now life. But thanks to the faith and life of simple people, the corridors are now much more brightly lit.

I did not really do anything special—except to open my eyes and ears to the sounds and sights of real life. Sharing life with other people, I entered the real world of people and events today as well as the real world of the people in the Bible. I discovered that while these two worlds are truly different, the lives of the people in them have the same roots and prompt the same questions. Life helped me to get a better understanding of the Bible, and the Bible helped me to gain a better understanding of life. In this book, which arose out of a series of talks in my neighborhood, I shall try to shed some light on life today by showing what the lives of the people in the Bible have to tell us.

7

"God, where are you?" Before we learn anything about God, we must know something of ourselves. We know that *we are here*. We feel that we know something about the path of life on which we are travelling. We are aware of the situation that prompts us to raise certain questions. It is the fact that *we are here* that prompts us to ask: "God, where are you?'' Our dialogue with God starts from the reality of our life here, and that is the point from which the reflections in this book start.

In the chapters of this book we shall consider aspects of the life of the people in the Bible, aspects that are still part of our lives today. We shall see how the people of the Bible, with their feet on the ground and their heads in the clouds, managed to sense and grasp the appeals of God that emanated from life. They took their cue from those appeals, pointed their lives in a certain direction, and, as a result, managed to arrive at the resurrection. Perhaps their example can help us to do the same today. Perhaps we too can hear the summons of God emanating from the reality around us, let it become an integral part of our own lives, and allow it to lead us to an authentic resurrection that is guaranteed by the resurrection of Jesus Christ. We shall consider features of life that posed questions to the people in the Bible long ago and that now pose questions to us. The people of the Bible found solid answers for those questions that still challenge us.

1

Paradise: Myth or Reality?

Difficulties in the Paradise Account

Present-day science propounds evolution as a highly probable hypothesis. The Bible, on the other hand, presents the creation of humanity as the direct work of God: "Then the Lord God formed a man from the dust of the ground" (Gn 2:7). Which is right?

In the first account of creation (Gn 1:26), man is the last to be created. In the second account of creation (Gn 2:7), man is the first to be created. How are we to explain this contradiction?

Many myths and legends of antiquity speak familiarly of a "tree of life" (Gn 2:9), a "serpent" (Gn 3:1), and a paradisiacal era at the beginning of time. Can the language of the Bible be regarded as mythical and legendary?

In Paradise there is a river that feeds four streams: the Tigris, the Euphrates, the Nile, and the Ganges (Gn 2:10–14). Where can we find a geographical point that would contain such a source?

11

How could God make all human misery depend on the sin of a single couple? How could woman be formed from the rib of a man? How could man be formed from "the dust of the ground" (Gn 2:7)?

Such questions arise in our minds because we, perhaps unwittingly, regard the Paradise account as providing *historical information.* We are of the opinion that the author wrote these verses in order to tell us something about the course of real events at the very start of human history. But this mental outlook, which lies behind our reading and evaluation of the Paradise account, does not correspond to the intention the author had when he put that data in writing.

The Viewpoint of the Biblical Author

The biblical author lived hundreds of thousands of years after the events he purports to describe. He was not at all interested in the past for its own sake, but he was deeply concerned about the situation in his own day. Something was wrong. The future seemed jeopardized, and something had to be done. That was the problem that preoccupied him and which led him to write his account. He was a thoroughgoing realist.

The intention of the biblical author, which will be explored in this chapter, can be summed up in five points: (1) He perceives the disastrous situation of his people and wants to denounce the evil in clear-cut terms. (2) He is not content with a general denunciation; he wants to point up where the responsibility lies. He wants the reader to discover the "origin" of the unfortunate situation, the evil that lies at the root of it all, the "original" sin. (3) Since people have lost sight of the responsibility involved, the author wants his description to raise the consciousness of his fellows regarding the blame that might be theirs. (4) The author wants to arouse them to action, so that they will tackle the evil at its roots and thus transform the unfortunate situation into a state of overall well-being. He is trying to effect what elsewhere in the Bible is called "conversion." (5) Finally, he wants to assure them that this transforming and practical action, and the will of God which serves as its guarantee, is greater than the force that maintains the evil situation. Thus he will awaken people's will to fight against the evil and help to instill hope and courage in them.

The Situation to Be Denounced

Perception of evil depends to some extent on the level of culture. Lack of water is a great evil for us, but it is not such a great evil for the Bedouin in the desert. Thus the biblical author perceives evil in accordance with his culture, his own level of awareness, and his sensitivity.

First of all, he notes a *general ambivalence in life:* (1) Human love, so good and beautiful in itself, has been turned into a tool for domination (Gn 3:16). Why? (2) The procreation of new offspring, designed to augment joy between human beings, entails the pangs of childbirth (Gn 3:16). Why? (3) One's own individual life is ambivalent. One wants to live and go on living, but death awaits (Gn 3:19). Why? (4) The earth is designed to produce nourishing food for human beings, but instead it produces only "thorns and thistles" (Gn 3:18). Why? (5) There is something incomprehensible about work, which is meant to provide us with the necessities of life. Much effort is expended for a very meager return (Gn 3:19). Why? (6) Enmity exists between human beings and other animals. Life is not safe and secure. Snakes are a real threat. Why does life combat life (Gn 3:15)? (7) God is our creator and friend, but in fact he is a cause for fear (Gn 3:10). Why?

The biblical author also testifies to the existence of an *extraordinary amount of violence.* Cain slays Abel. One individual fights with another, taking vengeance seventy-seven times (Gn 4:24). There is also a diminution in the life of faith, which is now little more than ritual and an admixture of magic and superstition. The divine and the human are confused (Gn 6:1–2). Finally the biblical author sees a total disintegration of humanity. People do not understand each other; they are always fighting with each other and trying to get the upper hand. People live on the defensive in a state of siege (Gn 11:1–9).

This is the situation the author ascertains around him: complete chaos. The majority of his contemporaries do not understand this situation and even help to compound the confusion. The biblical author wants to awaken others to the danger that is facing them if they continue along the same lines. He is basically a "nonconformist." Why?

He is convinced that the blame cannot be placed on God. Nor does he think it is right to say: "Relax, we'll manage somehow. It is God's will." He would be the last person in the world to look to God or religion for some way to justify a false patience that only worsens the present state of affairs. His faith tells him that God does not will the present state of affairs. And so he is faced with two questions: How would God like the world to be? If the world is not what God would like it to be, then who is responsible for the mess that exists? His faith in God makes him an aware and conscientious person who simply cannot accept the present situation. It prompts him to resist, to look for some solution, and to raise the consciousness of others to the same level that he is operating on. His feeling is: "If God does not want things to be this way, then I must not do anything that will perpetuate the world as it is."

Paradise As God's Ideal

The biblical author himself does not know how the world ought to be either. But he does know that God is good, just, and truthful. He thus imagines a situation in direct opposition to the one he knows first hand. It is a situation of thoroughgoing well-being: Paradise.

This Paradise is described by the author (Gn 2:4–25): (1) The wife is no longer dominated by her husband; she is his equal and companion (Gn 2:22–24). (2) Life goes on forever because a tree of life exists (Gn 2:9). (3) The land produces trees and fruit in abundance, and there is no desert (Gn 2:8–9). (4) Work is not oppressive but easy; its yield is abundant because it is easy to take care of a garden with flowering trees (Gn 2:15). (5) The fertility of the soil is guaranteed by an abundance of water than cannot be found on any part of the present-day earth (Gn 2:10–14). (6) Instead of being hostile to people, other animals obey and serve them (Gn 2:19–20). (7) God is the friend and intimate companion of human beings; God takes walks and engages in conversation with them (Gn 3:8). (8) There is no violence, no magical abuse of divine things, no abusive domination of others.

It is a picture and a situation of total harmony: of God with human beings, of one human being with another, of human beings with the world of animals and nature. Complete order prevails, in direct contrast to the chaos the author sees and experiences in his day-to-day life. There is no ambivalence whatsoever.

That is what God wants. Paradise is, as it were, the model of the world that God wants. God entrusted his construction plans to us so that we could fashion our own happiness. It was really possible for us to live forever and be immortal, to be happy and devoid of suffering, and to live in harmony with God and be sinless. Indeed it still *is* really possible because God has not changed his mind. God still wants that Paradise.

That Paradise should exist. In describing it the biblical author denounces the world he knows. Enlightened by the author's description, the reader is then led to ask certain questions that mark the first step on the road to "conversion": If that is the case, then why is the world exactly the opposite of what it should be? Who is responsible? The author's response to this question is provided by his account of "original sin."

Responsibility for Evil

The author speaks a language that is alien to us but that was quite clear and realistic for the people of his own day. The command not to eat of the fruit of "the tree of the knowledge of good and evil" may seem arbitrary to us. For the biblical writer and his people, however, the wisdom that served as a guide through life was often represented by the image of a tree. Wisdom told us what was good and evil, informing us whether a given course of action led towards fullness of life with God or not. God himself had given this knowledge through *the law*. If human beings chose to determine on their own what led to life (good) and what did not lead to life (evil), they would find anything but life; they would meet death. Thus the prohibition in the Genesis account speaks against those people who have chosen not to follow the law of God any longer but rather to decide for themselves what the criterion of moral behavior in life is. It speaks against those who have set themselves up as the sole and absolute criterion, who no longer regard life as a gift and a duty but rather as their own exclusive possession having no connection or relationship with any value outside themselves.

For the biblical author, the law of God is the instrument of order and progress. Observance of this law enables us to attain peace and to fashion Paradise. Disorder is rooted in the fact that his contemporaries have been disregarding this law, this declaration of human rights and duties. The forbidden fruit is the abusive use of liberty against God, and hence against human beings themselves.

What was the cause of this? Why were human beings abandoning this basic orientation in their lives? The cause was *the serpent* and his lures. The serpent was the symbol of the Canaanite religion, an agreeable religion entailing cultic ritual of a sexual nature and devoid of ethical commitments. It demanded little more than the observance of certain rites. This religion was a great temptation for the Hebrew people. It invited them to take refuge in easy ritual and to give up the harsh exigencies of the law. For the biblical author, the sin of his people was concretely rooted in that temptation.

Through this presentation the biblical author prodded his contemporaries to make a serious re-examination of their lives. Their world could be different if they did not follow this "serpent." Thus the biblical author was not thinking primarily of what had taken place in the distant past; he was thinking of what was going on around him, and perhaps even within himself. His account is a public confession of guilt. "Adam" and "Eve" can be translated as "a man" and "a woman" representing all. They are a mirror offering a critical reflection of contemporary reality and thus helping people to see in themselves the mistake pointed up in Adam and Eve. They should not ask: "Why are we all suffering because of one man and one woman?" The purpose of the account is not to allow people to shift the blame to others. It is to get the readers to admit that they act like that, that all of us share responsibility for the evil that exists. The biblical author is not a sentimentalist lamenting the good old days. He wants everyone to wake up to their personal responsibilities, to tackle the roots of evil in themselves. They can overcome this evil because God wills that they do so.

The author's description of the origin of evil does not end with this description of the "original sin." The initial error is only the beginning of the disgraceful mess: (1) Abusing liberty, humankind detaches itself from God and then from each other. Cain kills Abel, Cain representing all those who mistreat or kill their fellow human beings. (2) There is an alarming increase in violence, and vengeance is multiplied many times over (Gn 4:24). (3) Now separated from both God and fellow humans, humankind goes on the defensive; it looks to flight and rite and magic for salvation (Gn 6:1–2). Pursuing this line of conduct, humanity eventually grows obdurate and starts to disintegrate. It becomes impossible for people to live together and act in common (the tower of Babel). Despite all this, the biblical author is hopeful. He foresees victory over the evil that stems from the serpent (Gn 3:15).

The Author's Solution

It is humanity that is responsible for everything. Hence we should not simply be revolted by evil, of whatever sort it may be; we should also struggle and fight to bring about its disappearance. We have the mission and the capacity to do this because God wills it. Paradise continues to exist as *a real possibility* because God did not destroy it. God simply placed an angel before the entrance in order to halt our improper advance (Gn 3:24). The future is still open.

Speaking in popular terms, the author shows that God has not abandoned humankind. God makes clothes for the couple (Gn 3:21), protects Cain (Gn 4:15), and saves Noah from the flood caused by humanity's evil (Gn 6:9–9:17). When humanity eventually disintegrates to the point where joint action is no longer possible, God summons Abraham in order to reach all others through him (Gn 12:1–3). Thus begins salvation history.

The human grouping that begins with Abraham

might be considered "God's party" in the world.
This group believes it is possible to eliminate evil
with the power of God, to transform the world and
fashion a Paradise of total peacefulness. Its roots are
solid and true because it lives with God (Gn 17:1–2).
It eliminates opposition and forms a people, the
"people of God" (Ex 20:1–7). It does not exercise
domination, nor is it protected for that purpose. Its
purpose is service, and that is why it is called a
"kingdom of priests" and a "holy nation" (Ex 19:5).
The readers of the biblical account are members of
this people. The author wants them to realize what
it means to belong to the people of God. This people
must be active in the world, recognizing the true
meaning and purpose of life and carrying life forward by resistance to evil and transformation of
existing conditions. It keeps up its hope, which is
guaranteed by God's will for good.

With the coming of Jesus Christ, God's plan took
on concrete form. Paradise became a fact in Jesus'
resurrection. That is why Paul regards Jesus as a
"new Adam" (see Rom 5:12–19), and why the author of the book of Revelation describes the future
awaiting us in images derived from the earthly
Paradise (see Rv 21:4; 22:2–3).

Response to the Difficulties

Is the Paradise account myth or reality? It is reality insofar as it talks about the destiny of humanity.
The harmony described in the Paradise account is a

real possibility, guaranteed by the power of God that was manifested in the resurrection of Jesus Christ. It is myth insofar as the author used the mythical language and imagery of his day to express and transmit this reality to his readers.

Is it historical or merely a figment of the author's imagination? There is no reason to think that any Paradise once existed in the terms described in Genesis 2:4–25. What existed then, and still continues to exist today, is the real possibility for us to realize perfect harmony and peace when we allow ourselves to be guided by God's light and power. It makes no sense to ask: "Why didn't God give Adam and Eve a second chance?" God is continually offering this second chance to humanity, right up to our own day. The problem does not lie with God or with Adam and Eve. It is our problem now. Paradise will exist, will become a "historical" reality, when we will it and work for it. The only expedition that will ever be able to discover Paradise is the one that sets out resolutely for a better future.

The Bible says nothing positively or negatively about evolution. The Bible is rather concerned with the human problem and seeks to offer us God's view of life. There is neither contradiction nor agreement between the two accounts of man's creation (Gn 1:26, man created last; and Gn 2:7, man created first). These are two different narratives, each with its own objective.

What about the river that feeds the four major

streams in the world of that age (Gn 2:10–14)? It is a literary device to express the ideal fertility of the earth. The formation of man from the dust of the ground is another literary image designed to show that in God's hands, man is like a piece of clay in the hands of a potter: He is wholly dependent on God and very fragile in himself (see Jer 18:6). The formation of woman from the rib of man is a concrete way of visualizing a popular Hebrew saying: "bone from my bones" (Gn 2:23). It is a way of explaining the divine origin and mystery of sexual attraction, which we should not abuse.

What about the serpent as the concretization of the devil? This is mentioned in the book of Wisdom (2:24). Humankind's original error was the abuse of liberty, disobedience of God's law as expressed in the ten commandments.

What concrete form did that first sin take? No one knows, and the Bible does not say. What the Bible does tell us is that at the time the author was putting together his final narrative, the root evil took the concrete form of succumbing to the false religion of the Canaanites. We today must do what the biblical author did. We must look around us to see what concrete form is being taken by that "original sin," what today is the "serpent" enticing us to be unfaithful to God and human beings.

If the biblical author were alive today, his description would be quite different. He would closely scrutinize our present-day situation, try to pinpoint

the source of contemporary evils, and then probably offer a different description of the ideal world.
For example, he might present it as a developed
nation in which everyone was paid an adequate
wage and worked a forty-hour week; in which all
owned their own home, shared the profits of economic enterprise, and knew how to read and write.
In this modern Paradise social and individual
well-being would take complete priority over greed
for profit. There would be no exploitation or violence or foreign domination. There would be no
speeding or accidents on the highway, no slums or
shantytowns, no generation gap or educational
problems. Life and safety would be a sure thing, so
that there would be no need for the army or police.
In short, the world would be in complete harmony,
very different from what it is now.

This Paradise should exist. It *is* possible to con-
struct such a future. And so we are faced with the
same questions that were posed to the readers of
the Genesis account: Why isn't the world like that?
What stops our progress toward such a future?
Who or what is responsible? How are we to act so
that the world can be transformed into the world as
it should be? The Bible thus attempts to raise questions that are far more serious and complex than
questions of a purely historical nature. But historical questions have distracted us, alienating us from
our present-day reality.

Conclusion

The biblical description of Paradise is a public confession, a manifesto of opposition, a cry of hope, and a summons to transform the existing world.

The author does not "prove" the existence of an "original sin." He simply verifies its existence and tries to determine what form it is taking in his own day. He is not concerned about elaborating a theory as to how evil entered the world; he is trying to present a strategy for getting it out of the world.

The doctrine of original sin was later clarified by Paul (Rom 5:12–19; 1 Cor 15:21 22). Sin affects us down to our very roots, but it does not eliminate our capability of doing good. Insofar as our personal sins multiply, we ratify that original sin. We eat the forbidden fruit and add to the "culpable" evils of humanity. Future generations will inherit the evil we have helped to maintain and intensify.

Baptism makes us capable of facing up to evil. It involves us with that group of people who believe in God's plan and who are trying to carry it out in history; they hope in God and expect God to help them in and through Jesus Christ.

2

Abraham: Man in Search
of the Absolute

Difficulties Surrounding the
Figure of Abraham

Genesis 12–25 deals with Abraham. His life was not an easy one, but he enjoyed the advantage of having God close by his side. God stepped in, spoke to him, and gave direction to Abraham's life. But what about today? Where is that same God? Has God changed or have we become worse?

If the story of Abraham is merely meant to offer me an example upon which to reflect as I try to draw conclusions about my own life, then I would prefer to recall such figures as Pope John XXIII, Martin Luther King, Jr., and Mahatma Gandhi. These people were closer to *my* life here and now. Abraham lived in a totally different situation.

Moreover, Christ has already come. Abraham prepared the way for his coming. Why should we continue to focus our attention on the old when the new has already arrived? After all, when the building is finished we take away the scaffolding.

There is also the danger we might use our purported concern with the life of Abraham as a subterfuge and an excuse for nonaction. Confusing such concern with an interest in religion, we might talk ourselves into believing that we are good people who are carrying out our duties. In reality we may be completely failing to do what has to be done to change the world for the better.

These questions and difficulties are serious ones. They call into question the usefulness of the figure of Abraham for us today. How can the ancient texts really help us to solve our present-day problems and find God in the reality of everyday life? We repeat what was said earlier regarding the Paradise account: Our customary way of approaching the figure of Abraham does not correspond with the aim which the biblical author had in mind.

The Bible's Viewpoint on Abraham

To offer an example here, consider how we Brazilians celebrate our political independence during the *semana de Pátria*. We commemorate the famous cry of independence raised by Dom Pedro by the Ipiranga River. It is recounted in the history books children read at school and commemorated in the Ipiranga monument in São Paulo. During

Independence Week, newspapers reprint the full text of the revolutionary manifesto.

These are varied ways of commemorating one and the same fact. If we consider them closely, we will soon realize that none of them gives a precise version of the original fact itself, which is lost in the obscurity of past history. People have different opinions as to what actually happened back then.

History books try to give the more likely version of what actually happened. The Ipiranga monument shows us the importance that the fact had for those who constructed the monument. Our celebration of Independence Week and our reprinting of the manifesto indicated different ways of interpreting the same event. The cry of Dom Pedro began something which, though small in itself, is highly prized by Brazilians. It marked the start of political liberty and independence. Our commemorations and celebrations are not interested in the fact itself but in the meaning it has for our lives.

Picture a monument that had been constructed section by section over a long period of time. Since its various sections had been added at different points in history, the end result would be a heterogenous affair that did not seem to be all of one piece. Each part would tell us something about the vision of freedom and independence held by those responsible for that particular section. The biblical narratives about Abraham are very much like that.

Abraham lived somewhere around 1800–1700 B.C. With him began something which may have been small in itself, but which the Hebrew people came to value more and more. The descendants of Abraham recorded and celebrated this basic fact in accordance with the significance that it had for their own lives. As each succeeding century went by, descriptions were elaborated to fit the outlook of those living at the time. Finally, in the fifth century B.C., someone worked up the final edition of the story we now find in the Bible. It contains elements from four previous descriptions, as scholarly science has documented over the past fifty or sixty years. Thus the biblical narrative on Abraham is disconnected and heterogenous.

It is therefore difficult for us to know exactly what happened, because the Bible is not interested in that. The biblical writers wanted to present the figure of Abraham to the people of their day in such a way that they could learn from him how they might discover God and journey with God through life.

But doesn't this amount to a falsifying of history? No, not really. You can take a snapshot photo of someone or you can take an x-ray. The photographic plates will reveal two completely different things. Most history books try to take photographs of past facts and events. The Bible takes x-rays of the same events. Though different, the two sets of pictures are authentic.

Moreover, the full import and scope of an event is

not always appreciated when the event is actually taking place. Only at a distance, over a long period of time, does the event show up clearly. When you start to round a big curve, you do not always notice the size of the curve at first. Only later can you look back and see how much of a curve it was and where it began. When Abraham started on the "curve" that would change his whole life, he himself probably did not pay too much attention to it. But later, when the Hebrew people looked back from a distance, they became aware of the fact that their existence as a nation belonging to God began back there with Abraham. The Bible does not describe the event as Abraham lived it, but rather as the Hebrew people saw it much later in and through the problems of each succeeding age.

Abraham's Life

These remarks may raise a question in the reader's mind: What, then, was Abraham's life really like? What exactly happened when God entered our life? What was the concrete happening in which the Hebrew people experienced the start of God's active intervention? Knowing the answer to such questions will help us take an x-ray of our lives and thus find the signs of God's presence and involvement with us.

We know Abraham lived in approximately the nineteenth or eighteenth century before Christ.

At God's bidding he left Ur of the Chaldees (in present-day Iraq, near the Persian Gulf) and went up as far as the city of Haran in Assyria (present-day Syria). Then he came down to Palestine, continued on to Egypt, and finally returned to Palestine. There he died in the town of Hebron. Abraham was in continuing contact with God, and he acted upon God's bidding. This is clear to anyone who reads the pertinent chapters in Genesis (12–25).

Here two factors should be mentioned that will clarify the matter from a historical point of view. (1) In those days there was a large migratory movement that brought people from the Persian Gulf area up through Syria and then down to Palestine and Egypt. Abraham was one of those many migrants, indistinguishable from the rest. (2) All the peoples and tribes involved in these migrations in search of better land had gods of their own. They were "family gods" for the most part, and everything done by those peoples was done at the bidding of their gods.

Looking at the facts from outside, then, one might be inclined to draw the conclusion that Abraham was in no way different from the other migrants, not even in terms of his faith, that he was just another face in the crowd.

What did those people of antiquity mean when they spoke of "God"? What type of God was it: the God of the Bible or another god? To some extent at

least, the religion shared by all those desert peoples
had grown up in the following manner: It was evident that life depended on harmony in nature and
the universe. Welcome rain came in the spring; the
seasons followed their regular cycle each year; the
animal herds were replenished when the animals
went into heat; a plentiful supply of water irrigated
the fields; and the continuing round of sun and
moon, day and night, helped to ensure life from
day to day. People could find in nature the things
they needed for subsistence. It was obvious, however, that life was constantly threatened by unpredictable forces: storms, floods, diseases. People
realized that it was impossible for them to exert
much influence over those forces for harmony or
those for disorder. The forces were stronger than
the people, and the people did not have any explanation for them. People came to feel that those
forces were unearthly or divine. If life was to continue, the forces would have to be beneficent. People thus began to worship those forces, and religion
came into being. Hence if people wanted to live a
decent and secure life *as human beings*, they would
have to honor the gods. Woe to those who did not!
They would jeopardize their own life and that of
others, because the gods might grow irritated and
stop maintaining the forces of harmony and order.

Those "gods" were not God in fact. They were
expressions of fear and hope, of the desire to go on
living. The worship rendered to the gods was an

expression of *the will to succeed and prosper in life.*
Abraham was a sincere human being, an authentic
man of his own day. He sought to prosper in life by
worshipping the God he had inherited from his
father (see Judith 5:7).

Today science has destroyed that ancient outlook
on harmony and disorder in the universe. These
realities are not the result of divine forces. The sun
does not rise because God pulls it up in the sky. Our
whole view of the matter has changed, thanks to
modern science. But one thing has not changed. *We
still have a perduring wish to succeed and prosper in life.*
Human beings still want to preserve life, to be faithful, to do what their consciences bid them. In
Abraham's day people did this by worshipping various divinities and using cultic magic. Today many
people still do the same looking for anything that
might give meaning to their lives.

Abraham was looking for an ideal in life, for some
absolute value. He was searching for something that
would have supreme value, so that everything else
would be relative by comparison. And he sought
this value in the realm of religious living, as many
people still do today. In our day, however, there are
also people who look elsewhere for such a value.
They do not consider religion, or God, or any divine
element. Instead they put value on their work to
benefit their family, on their efforts to build a more
humane world, or on their professional life as a
doctor, lawyer, or whatever.

Our conviction is that this is the way we find fulfillment in life and prosper as human beings. The basic preoccupation is still the same, even though it may concretize itself quite differently today. In Abraham's day people related in a vertical way with "the deity." Today many people have a horizontal relationship with "humanity." They want to work for others and to contribute to the welfare of all.

God's Entry into Life

In telling us how God entered Abraham's life, the Bible focuses a strong x-ray beam on our own lives. It shows us the precise point where God breaks through into the life of a human being. It tells us that God enters life and reveals himself to us precisely when and where we make a conscious effort *to be real human beings*, i.e., to fulfill the ideal proposed. That is precisely how God entered the life of Abraham.

This breakthrough is hardly perceptible at the start. God, traveling incognito, gets on the bus of life and pays his fare. He shoulders his way through the standing passengers and strikes up a conversation with Abraham. God does not walk up with a business card, announce that he is the Creator, and then spell out everything he wants done. Instead he dons a disguise, sidles in, and gradually wins a place in Abraham's life.

The ancient deities were generally projections of

humankind's deepest fears and desires. In and through the concrete forms that life took, the outline and visage of *Someone* took concrete form. Abraham and his people came to perceive an *active presence* in and beyond those forms. It was not identical with the forms themselves, and it gradually made its presence known and felt by the weight of its own evidence. No longer was it a deity that was basically dependent on human beings. It was Someone on whom human beings depended. Gradually, as time went on, this Someone would correct our ways of living. Abraham had now started out on a wide and decisive curve whose full dimensions would be discerned only much later by the Hebrew people. In and through the forms of worship people used to honor the impersonal divine forces, there gradually appeared the lineaments of the true God. The latter grew out of the former, much as a flower blooms from the bud.

The great lesson to be learned from all this is one that answers an important human question: Where is God? Where can I find God? The answer is that God enters human life and lets himself be discovered wherever human beings are trying to be faithful to themselves and others, wherever they are looking for an absolute value and trying to live it. It is there that we too must look for God today. It is there that we must try to discern the features of this *Someone* in whom we believe. God is not to be found first and foremost in cultic worship. Our worship has value only insofar as it embodies what we are living in our day-to-day lives.

Abraham accepted this presence and allowed it to have an influence on his life. Seen from the outside, nothing apparently had changed. On the inside, however, a light had begun to shine. Gradually it would begin to cast its glow all around, illuminating every corner of the universe. People would come to see that this *Someone* is God, the Creator of heaven and earth. That is why the figure of Abraham was so important and meaningful for those who would come after him.

But if all that went so unnoticed at the beginning, then how does one explain the constant dialogue between God and Abraham that is recounted in the Bible? Well, dialogue is communication established between two people, and it can take countless forms. When a married man takes a trip, he takes things with him that remind him of his wife. There is a dialogue between them because of the *presence* of his wife in his life. Only he senses and appreciates this presence, because only he lives in the friendship and love shared between him and his wife. When you love someone, everything around you can evoke recollections of that person. The dialogues put in terms of human language in the Bible are concrete expressions of the feelings that the Hebrew people had for God. They lived in friendship with him, and the dialogues helped to express what they had perceived about him. When people accept the presence of God in their lives and believe in him, then dialogue is established that has its own laws. It may seem strange to someone on the outside, but it is perfectly understandable to the person who is living in the presence of God.

When we read the story of Abraham, we see a human being just like us. He too is trying to prosper in life. In and through this effort he came to encounter the true God. But God was no closer to Abraham than he is to us today. Why, then, do we not encounter God today? Perhaps it is because our sight is bad. We are so preoccupied with a particular image of God that we feel that something else cannot possibly be God. Our receiving set is not tuned to the same wavelength that God is using to send out his summons. The God who revealed himself to Abraham, our God, is a God of human beings. Moreover, he is not afraid to hide himself. You may not see a butterfly when you are out hunting eagles; you may overlook the flowers if you are looking for trees.

God is present and reveals himself in many things: in a mother's dedication to her family, in the labor of a working man for his children, in the struggle of young people to create a more humane world, in the joy produced by the presence of a friend, and in the mutual interchange of understanding and consolation. It is in such things that we discover the presence of God and gradually trace the lineaments of his face.

Conclusions

God enters the life of a human being silently. He enters calmly and quietly through the ordinary events of everyday life. It is there that he reveals himself and his presence to those who have eyes to see him. When a person finally takes note of God's presence, God has probably been there a long time already. But then why does the Bible depict God's entrance into Abraham's life as a brusque and almost violent affair (Gn 12:1–4)? The reason is that it is easier to see the beginning of the curve, and the about-face it requires, from a distance. Even though God enters a human life imperceptibly, the fact is that he wants a total "conversion," a complete break with the past, a transformation of one's life.

God presents himself as Abraham's future: "I will fulfill my covenant between myself and you and your descendants after you . . . to be your God . . . " (Gn 17:7). Abraham, in other words, is to give up the other deities he had been following in his search for a prosperous life. The God of the covenant will be his guarantee of success. Thus God's entrance into Abraham's life confronts him with an either/or option. He must abandon the gods of the past and choose God alone (monotheism). If Abraham agrees to follow this new God, then he must travel the road of life as this God wants him to travel it (the ethical aspect of revealed religion); and his future will be assured by the fidelity and power of this God (hope in the future, messianism).

The difficult thing is to accept God's conditions and walk in faith. Abraham is presented to us as a man who did just that. He had to leave his homeland in order to obtain a new homeland, but he owned little more than a burial plot when it came time for him to die. He had to give up his family and native people in order to become the father of a new nation, but at the time of his death he had only one son. At the time that God promised him a large posterity, Abraham did not have any children and it did not seem that he would be able to have any. It was hard to believe in God's word because there was little proof. Then Isaac was born, and God eventually asked Abraham to sacrifice him. Abraham was ordered to kill the one and only hope he had of becoming the father of a great nation. But Abraham was willing to do that, to rely wholly on the word of God (Gn 22:1–18; Heb 11:19).

God's attitude seems to be contradictory at times. He promises Abraham a large posterity, then orders him to kill his only son. He bids Abraham leave his homeland for another, yet Abraham did not gain a real homeland while he was alive. At the same time Abraham, through his faith and his absolute confidence in God, became God's close friend and confidant (Gn 18:17–19).

This description of the figure of Abraham is not meant to correspond to the real life of Abraham, but rather to the ideal of faith in the era of the biblical author. This was how his fellow Hebrews must live if they were to be worthy members of the nation founded by Abraham.

Response to the Difficulties

Where is God? As the exposition in the preceding pages would indicate, the story of Abraham is meant to provide us with an answer to that question. The story does not allow us to draw many conclusions about our own life today, or even about Abraham's life. Its purpose is to invite and encourage the reader to be another Abraham, to truly make the effort to prosper in life, to be sincere with self and others so that one may discover the active presence of God.

Christ has already come, it is true. But he has not yet come for many people, perhaps not even for us. No one lives wholly in and with Christ. The important thing today is that people find out how they are to live, so that they can find their complete fulfillment in Christ. The story of Abraham tells us how to do that. The first step is to live a sincere life, to love truth, and honestly to seek the absolute: "All who are not deaf to truth listen to my voice" (Jn 18:37; see Jn 3:17–21; 8:44–45). If people take that pathway in life, then they will encounter the face of God.

The aim of the biblical account is not to have us analyze the story of Abraham solely in terms of historical happening, to find out how he actually lived and rest content with that. In seeking out answers to difficulties and problems of a historical nature, we are faced with other difficulties that are far more complex and important. Do I look for God where he allows me to find him, or do I prefer to stay somewhere where it will be very hard to find him? Do I look for God in real life or elsewhere? If other people know nothing about God, are we Christians not guilty of failing to reveal the true face of God to them in and through our own lives?

3

Exodus: God in the History of Liberation

Difficulties Surrounding the Exodus Story

The story of the Exodus seems to be one continuing miracle from beginning (the call of Moses) to end (the crossing of the Jordan after forty years of wandering in the desert). Without denying the reality of the miracle, one must admit that it seems strange we do not run into similar miracles today when so many people and nations need the same sort of liberation. Has God changed or have we become worse? Where is the miracle?

We believe in a liberator God. But where is he today? Liberty is dying in the hearts of human beings, of both the rich and the poor, for a variety of reasons that we ourselves have helped to produce. Where is our God and his liberty?

Many people have grown tired of waiting hopefully and have moved into action designed to bring about liberation. We have seen this happen in

Czechoslovakia, Hungary, Vietnam. We have seen it happen among blacks in the United States. National Liberation Fronts have sprung up as workers and others on the margin of society take cognizance of their situation and move toward concrete action. Does all that have something to do with our God? People involved in such movements usually prescind completely from God. They don't think about him, and they don't seem to have any need of him.

The following accusation is often levelled against Christians: You say that you are free, when in reality you are bound by laws and traditions that have been imposed by your so-called liberator God. You talk about liberty but you don't display it in your own lives. You are like poor bums who go around claiming to be the descendants of a Roman emperor. We, on the other hand, are truly free because we have liberated ourselves from that God of yours. Of what advantage or use is it to believe in your liberator God?

These are serious questions and difficulties. They raise problems about what the Exodus account has to say concerning the process of liberation.

The Bible's Viewpoint on the Exodus

There are many descriptions of the Exodus in the Bible. We find them in various books (Exodus, Numbers, Deuteronomy, and Wisdom 10–19;

Psalms 78, 105, 106, and 135; and in passages of the prophetic books, particularly Isaiah 40–55).

However, the various books that recall the Exodus event were written by different people at different points in history. Every sort of literary genre is used to describe the Exodus: prose and poetry, history and prophecy, hymn and narrative, liturgical text and wisdom literature. This would suggest that we are dealing with an event that was of the utmost importance in the life of the Hebrew nation. They recounted it and commented on it throughout their history. What was the reason for this great and perduring interest in the Exodus?

We can uncover this reason if we look at the many ways in which they spoke of the Exodus. In their descriptions of the event we find certain particular features that call for some consideration and explanation. First, there are frequent repetitions in the book of Exodus itself, and some incidents are recounted twice: the story of the manna, the quail, and the water struck from a rock; the call of Moses; the handing down of the decalogue. Second, there are obvious exaggerations in the accounts of the Exodus at various points: for example, in the poetic song of Exodus 15 and in the account of the plagues in the book of Wisdom. Third, we are faced with disconcerting uncertainties—about the plagues for example. Psalm 78 recounts seven plagues, Psalm 105 recounts eight plagues, and the book of Exodus mentions ten plagues. We also know that the book

of Exodus was composed from three older traditions that did not agree on the number of the
plagues. The Yahwist account, dating from the
tenth century, had seven plagues; the Elohist account, dating from between the ninth and eighth
century, had five plagues; and the Priestly account,
dating from between the sixth and fifth century,
had five plagues that do not correspond to the five
enumerated in the Elohist account. Fourth, the
miraculous aspect of the whole event is gradually
accentuated with the passage of time. The Yahwist
account says that only water drawn from the Nile
turned to blood (Ex 4:9); the Elohist account says
that all the water of the Nile turned to blood (Ex
7:20); and the Priestly account says that all the water
in Egypt turned to blood (Ex 7:19). Much later the
book of Wisdom, composed around the first century before Christ, will say even more fantastic
things about the plagues.

So what were the plagues in reality? It seems that
the author or final editor of the book of Exodus
decided that ten was a good number. But what
really happened? How exactly did water turn to
blood? Is it possible to find out how things really
happened?

These peculiar literary details, uncovered by
modern exegesis, indicate that the biblical authors
had certain basic concerns and a particular viewpoint. The basic concern is not primarily to narrate
history and give a journalistic report of what hap-

pened during the Exodus. The primary concern in describing the event is to convey its import for the life of the people, a life constantly evolving. The biblical account is not a description of the event; it is an *interpretation* of it. Hence in reading the Bible we cannot accept everything as literal fact, because that would involve us in contradictions. The biblical account itself is not primarily interested in the material aspect, nor does it take everything literally; for the various accounts reveal repetitions, exaggerations, and uncertainties.

The basic point in which the Bible is interested, the sense that it derives from the facts of the Exodus, is that in the Exodus God revealed himself to the Hebrew people and imposed himself on them as their God. This contact resulted in a commitment by the Hebrew people: the commitment of the covenant. In its description of the event, the Bible wants to bring out this divine dimension and to show that God was present and operative in the Exodus events. This helps to explain why the miraculous aspect was stressed as time went on. It was a suitable way of helping the reader to realize that there was a divine dimension at work.

An example may help to clarify this point. History books are like photographs; they describe what might be seen with the naked eye. The Bible is like an x-ray; on the exposed plate we find things that cannot be seen with the naked eye. On our own we cannot see or touch the operative presence of God

(Jn 1:18), but the x-ray of faith perceives and reveals God's presence. The viewpoint of the historians is different from that of the Bible. Their instruments of observation and measurement are not the same, and hence the results of their inquiry are different. While their results do not contradict one another, they are different aspects of one and the same reality. The biblical description tries to present the facts in such a way that the readers will see the divine dimension in the past and thus be able to perceive and shoulder responsibility for the divine dimension in what is taking place around them. Hence if the readers are to grasp the message of the Bible, they must try to develop the same outlook the author had in describing and presenting events.

Modern Science and the Bible

Adopting a historian's perspective and applying the criteria of modern scholarship to the Bible, we obtain a more accurate historical knowledge of the events that actually took place. This has been done, and we can conclude the following: The plagues were natural phenomena that took place in the Nile region. The crossing of the Red Sea was made possible by a low tide, which was helped along by a strong wind (Ex 14:21). The manna was some form of edible resin. These conclusions seem undeniable and certain, for such phenomena could occur in Egypt even today. Thus scientific scholarship can explain the events in purely natural terms and show that there was nothing extraordinary about them. What took place was a successful human attempt at liberation, like many others that have taken place before and after the time of Moses. At first glance such conclusions bewilder us.

The results of historical research, however, are in the category of photographs. The Bible does not deny them; it presupposes them as the basis for its x-ray analysis. It probes deeper and concludes that God was at work in the events described. Historical scholarship, for its part, cannot deny the conclusions of the Bible because such a denial would exceed its premises and the capabilities of its observational tools. The tools of scientific scholarship cannot register God's activity. God's presence is perceptible only to the person open to it in and through faith.

Thus the Bible shows a certain lack of concern and interest in the material aspect of events as history. Biblical authors give in to useless repetitions, exaggerations, and even contradictions. They add details or take away certain features, changing perspective as they deal with facts. It does not bother them to do this, for their main concern is to communicate the deeper message lying buried in the facts and events. The point of the Exodus account is that God was present and at work in that successful human effort at liberation. The biblical writer wants to open the eyes of his readers to what is happening around them in their own day. He wants us to realize that God is involved with the many liberation movements springing up around us today.

I cannot see microbes with the naked eye, but I can verify their existence and activity in the pains of a disease. And if I have the right instrument, I can even see them. Mere reasoning may not enable me to see the God of Exodus in today's world, but I can ascertain the results of his presence: people becoming freer, more human, more aware and responsible. And if I possess the proper instrument, that is, faith, I can see the sign of God's presence in all this.

What happened in the time of Moses is still happening today and will continue to happen throughout history. Events have a fourth dimension not visible to the naked eye. If people become overly impressed with one viewpoint on things, they may become insensitive to other possible viewpoints. If people are interested only in the "scientific" view of things, they may suffer a diminution in the ability to perceive the hidden aspect of things, to profit from the insights of literature, art, music, philosophy. When human beings lock themselves up inside their scientific achievements and their own selves, their openness to God may atrophy. Eventually they may cease to give any importance to the divine dimension of events that is revealed by faith. In many instances, however, the fault is not that of science or scholarship, but that of those who profess but do not really live the faith. The way they live their lives seems to prove that faith does not have much to contribute to the progress and growth of humanity.

Seen in this perspective, the Bible can be a light that will help us to discover the hidden divine dimension in our lives. To be specific, the Exodus account can reveal the operative presence of God in certain sectors of human life where we do not usually look for it.

The Divine Dimension of the Exodus

If we examine the Exodus event solely in terms of human criteria, we would have to say that it was a successful attempt to obtain liberation from the yoke of oppression that the Pharaoh had imposed on the Hebrews. It was a successful quest for freedom and independence, like that undertaken by many other people before and after Moses. People continue to seek the same liberation today because the yearning for liberty is a very powerful one.

The Bible looks at this same event in the light of faith. It relates the historical events, but it does not put its main stress on the material reality of the events that took place. Rather it stresses the concrete experience the people lived through and their unshakeable conviction that God was present and at work in it. The Bible views that struggle for liberation as a manifestation of God's presence among human beings and as the start of a journey that leads to Christ and his resurrection. Through its description the Bible draws a lesson that is meant to help us perceive the divine dimension in events taking place today. Where there is a sincere effort at liberation, be it group or individual, there we hear the friendly voice of our liberator God calling out to us. In such efforts lies the road leading human beings to Christ and the fullness of the resurrection.

But is it possible, we might ask, that the biblical view of the Hebrew people's liberation from Egypt was the result of group autosuggestion? That certainly is possible, but then how would one explain the results? I can deny the presence of microbes, but if I do then I must explain the illness in some other way. The results of the Exodus account are such that no explanation seems to be quite as satisfactory as the one offered by the Bible. In this particular case, historical scholarship finds it impossible to find one cause that will adequately explain the results. This seems to speak in favor of the authenticity of the interpretation offered by the people who lived through the events that were part of their liberation from Egypt.

The end result, which history can verify but cannot satisfactorily explain, is this: As the Hebrew people continued on in their journey toward liberation, they became freer and more responsible. They became more sensitive to human problems, more aware and more loving. They found more strength and courage to keep moving on the road of life, to keep their heads held high where others might have despaired. All this is stated in the Bible and verified by historical investigation. It was evident to the Hebrew people. They saw it as a consequence of the Exodus and as a by-product of God's activity. Now if this vision of life rendered such great service to human beings where other visions had failed, then it merits confidence. A real-life experience with God was at the origin of the Hebrew people, and it enabled them to attain their liberty. It hardly seems right to classify it as some form of group autosuggestion.

The Initial Episode of Liberation History

We find two currents running parallel in the history of the chosen people. On the one hand there is a growing awareness of oppression. You cannot liberate people who are unaware of the oppression under which they are living. They would not know what liberty is, and hence they could not avail themselves of it. Running parallel to this growing awareness of oppression, we find a progressive process of liberation. Once their consciousness has been raised regarding their situation, the people commit themselves to action on behalf of liberation. They see it as their inalienable task. The Bible makes it clear that both these currents have something to do with God.

In that sense the Exodus was just a starting point. Consciousness-raising began at the point where the oppression was most keenly felt. The people first noticed their cultural and political oppression. But the consciousness-raising work of God continued after the Exodus itself. Through his chosen leaders it continued to work on the people, moving toward the ultimate root of all oppression: egotism, which closes us up within ourselves and tempts us to create oppressive structures at every level of life.

The task of liberation did not stop either. Begun at the Exodus from Egypt, it continued on through the history of the chosen people. Finally, the root of oppression was eradicated through the liberating love preached by Jesus Christ. The true liberty that God envisions for humankind is that which is born of love for God and one's fellow human beings. The Exodus initiated by Moses reached its destination in the resurrection of Jesus Christ to true life. It is summed up in the Gospel message: "Whoever cares for his own safety is lost; but if a man will let himself be lost for my sake and for the Gospel, that man is safe" (Mk 8:35).

God has no need of our liberty. God is not interested in giving us liberty as if it were a present. God himself is free. It is contact with God that frees us and puts in our hearts the seed of true liberty.

This seed was sown in the hearts of the Hebrew people at the time of the Exodus, and it grew from there. They had lived in Egypt for a long time (Ex

12:40) before they realized the oppression from which they were suffering. Only when it became intolerable did they take cognizance of it and give expression to their desire for liberation (Ex 1:1–2:25). Then God responded to their plea, summoning Moses to carry out the task of liberation (Ex 3:7–10, 6:2–8).

Although the activity of God in the Exodus is greatly stressed, because the biblical writer sees events in the light of his fuller faith, the artifices used by Moses to obtain his objective are clearly brought out. The ruse was that the Hebrews wanted to make a three-day pilgrimage into the desert (Ex 5:1–3; 7:16; 9:1; 8:25–27). To avoid perilous encounters with Pharaoh's army, Moses led the people south toward the Red Sea (Ex 13:17–18). He managed to cross the river because a strong dry wind held back the tide (Ex 14:21) and whipped up a sandstorm in the desert so that the visibility of the Egyptians was hindered (Ex 14:19–20).

But all the stratagems of human calculation were not the most important thing. Most important for them and for us was the new faith that was born of that experience. The people came to believe that God was journeying with them and that Moses spoke to them as God's own interpreter (Ex 14:31). The biblical account seeks to stir up the same faith in its readers, to stimulate them to the same liberative effort, and to get them to celebrate God's liberative presence in their midst: "Sing to the Lord, for he has risen up in triumph'' (Ex 15:21). Thus the Exodus account sheds light on a journey which began in Egypt and which has not ended yet. It is the journey of us all towards the promised land where the full liberty of God holds sway.

This vision of life offers us a new perspective on the true import of the events that are taking place today. It is the concrete and careful plan of liberation that God has always made himself known to us and led us to Christ. Today this plan may take many varied forms. We overcome our personal limitations by work and study. We strive to overcome some vice or fault that is weighing down on us. We undergo psychotherapy to free ourselves of complexes and unfortunate conditionings. A doctor frees fellow human beings from the oppression of bodily ills, a teacher helps to overcome the ravages of illiteracy, a skilled technician teaches people how to take care of their health or plant a garden. Nations try to free themselves from colonialism and imperialism, workers unite to protect their rights, international bodies formulate declarations about the basic rights of human beings. People in general try to overcome all the varied forms of egotism, denounce injustice and torture, and promote international development. The awesome work of liberation takes countless forms.

In and through all these efforts the human race journeys painfully through its own Exodus in search of total liberty. We all have our own Exodus to make from childhood to adulthood, as does each societal group and nation. Humanity as a whole is immersed in its Exodus; as Vatican II put it, it is radically and wholly immersed in "the paschal mystery of Christ." In this whole process there is an opening through which God enters, makes this presence felt, and acts on behalf of human beings. We can find him there if we will. From the outside there is nothing special to be seen, but the eye of faith can discern the underlying divine dimension in everything that human beings suffer and live through.

Must we conclude, then, that everything done in the name of liberty is endorsed by God? Such a conclusion goes far beyond the premises. There are so-called liberation movements that actually lead to greater oppression because they produce hatred and egotistical concentration on the narrow interests of one particular group. How are we to distinguish them from authentic liberation movements? What is the criterion for proper discernment?

The Exodus Story as a Basis for Discernment

Moses was educated at the Pharaoh's court (Ex 2:5–10). It was customary in his day to do this with children of the nobility from occupied countries. They were brought to Egypt and educated there so that later they would serve the best interests of

Egypt. Moses did not follow through with this planned career. Revolting against the degrading situation in which his people found themselves, he slew an Egyptian soldier (Ex 2:11–12). The deed may well have been connected with an attempt at liberation that failed. In any case Moses had to flee (Ex 2:14–22). In exile God approached him a second time and bade him to return to Egypt and free his people (Ex 2:23–4:18). After putting up a great deal of resistance, Moses obeyed and undertook this mission.

The liberty for which he was now going to fight steadfastly was no longer defined in purely nega-tive terms, i.e., freedom from the political oppres-sion of the Pharaoh. It now had positive content as well. If people are fighting just to be *free from* something, then they know only what is *not* wanted. Lacking any criterion or standard to direct their action forward, they move into the future with their eyes turned backward. The liberty that now appeared on the horizon for Moses, however, was part of a larger plan that God had in mind: God meant to free the Hebrew people from Egypt so that they might be his people and he might be their God (Ex 6:6–8). The Hebrew people were to be free *for* something, free for a covenant with God. They would know what they did not want because they would know what they did want in life. They had a criterion for acting and moving into the future.

This objective would give direction to the activity

of Moses and the Hebrew people throughout their history. It would give solid content to the freedom for which they yearned. If something did not contribute toward this objective, then it would not really contribute to their liberty. Thus it is clear that God's entrance into the lives of human beings is a light that provides both correction and orientation. The first correction, or conversion, took place in the mind of Moses; he was turned from killing to consciousness-raising.

Not everything done in the name of liberty leads to the liberty that God has in mind for his people. By the same token, the effort to attain liberation does not always take place in a peaceful, nonviolent way. The first reaction to Moses' attempt at liberation was a hardening of heart on the part of the Pharaoh and intensified oppression of the Hebrew people (Ex 5:1–18). This in turn led the Hebrew people to revolt against Moses, since he had whipped up the Egyptians and given them further cause to kill the Hebrews (Ex 5:19–21). Moses protested the intensified oppression (Ex 5:22–6:1), but the Pharaoh only stiffened further (Ex 7:12, 22; 8:15–19; 9:7, 12, 35; 10:20, 27). Moses had to overcome the fear and apathy of his own people, to convince them that the stiffening of the Pharaoh was part of God's action to pave the way for their liberation (Ex 7:3–5; 9:35; 10:20, 27). The work of Moses essentially involved trying to make the Hebrew people aware of their oppression so that they would choose to work for liberation as a task imposed on them by God. Moses interpreted various signs and happenings as God's summons to his people and God's actions on their behalf. Moses let facts and events do the talking for him.

The Pharaoh finally gave in, and the Hebrew people started out from Egypt (Ex 12:37). They began the journey to liberation as a task willed by God. But that journey was, as it always is, an ambiguous one. On the very threshold of freedom everything seemed to fall apart. Cornered between the sea and the Egyptian army, the Hebrew people lost heart and rebelled against Moses (Ex 14:11-12). Moses appealed to their faith, the people continued forward, and freedom came into being (Ex 14:30). In that we see revealed the faith of the leader in the cause that he was defending and promoting. He saw it as a victorious cause. Moses was not the one who provoked the violence. It was the Pharaoh who did that because he did not want the Hebrew people to set out on the journey to freedom. It was much more convenient for him to have an enslaved people at his bidding.

Celebrating the Liberation Granted by God

The great experience of the Hebrew people was that God had liberated them and that they were his people (Ex 19:4-6). Everything that befell them was viewed in the light of that fundamental faith. God was present in everything, arranging for the good of his people. Human shrewdness led the fleeing Hebrews to choose the less dangerous route heading towards the Red Sea, but they saw in this the guidance of God (Ex 13:17–18). They saw the hand of God in the strong wind that blew all night and kicked up a covering cloud of sand (Ex 14:20–21). This phenomenon helped to reduce the tide on the one hand and to provide a covering smoke screen on the other. The natural plagues, which are customary in Egypt, helped to create a general climate of confusion that abetted the flight to freedom. Seen in the x-ray light of faith, however, they became a revelation of God's liberative activity on their behalf. The Hebrew people and their leader managed to grasp the "signs of the time" and to carry out the objective of God, using artifice and stratagem when necessary.

The Exodus occurred at Passover, which was a customary pastoral feast of spring. The blood of a lamb was sprinkled on the doorpost to ward off the influence of evil spirits. It was on the occasion of that feast that the Hebrew people left Egypt; or they may have left to celebrate it in the desert. In later years the Passover ceased to be a feast designed to combat evil spirits; it became a commemoration of the people's liberation. A reminder of what God had done on their behalf, it gave them another chance to make a personal commitment to the further work of liberation. It helped to keep alive their hope for complete liberation in the future. The Hebrew feast of Passover (Hebrew *pesah*) was called *pascha* in Greek. This is why the life of those who believe in God and his promise is sometimes called a "paschal" life. In other words, it is a life which involves a "passover" from oppression to liberation. The *pascha* of Christ was the authentic one because he passed over from death to enduring life with God, and it is there that we find true liberty.

The effort to achieve liberation, and a continuing concern to celebrate that victory, deeply marked the history of the Hebrew people and became its most characteristic feature.

4

Samson and Delilah:
Folklore or Something More?

Difficulties Surrounding the Story of Samson

The story of Samson occupies a relatively large place in the book of Judges (chapters 13 to 16), approximately one fifth of the whole book. It deals with his birth (Jgs 13), his marriage (Jgs 14), his exploits and battles with the Philistines (Jgs 15), and his tragic but glorious end (Jgs 16). It is one of those episodes in the Bible about which we don't know exactly what to think.

Samson's attitudes did not conform to moral and ethical norms. Instead he did not seem to have any such norms; he followed his own impulses: the Bible mentions three women he was fond of. He killed people without the slightest scruple. His exploits and quarrels, most of them connected with love affairs, discomfited both his fellow countrymen and their enemies. Samson did what he pleased and acted in accordance with the way he personally saw things. Is it really possible that the Bible can see the Spirit of God at work in his way of using force? What are we to think of the whole story? Wouldn't it be better suited to an X-rated movie? It could be unwise and even dangerous to imitate Samson, and yet the Church continues to read the story of Samson today. Of what real use is it to us?

The Viewpoint of the Biblical Author

The book of Judges, written many years after the events it describes, is a patchwork quilt. The author constructs a new building out of old bricks. The final editor or author of the book of Judges lived in the seventh century B.C., at a time when many people were talking about the need for thorough-going reforms in the life of the Hebrew nation. (This whole reform movement will be discussed in greater detail in chapter 6 below). Many people felt there would be complete chaos unless such reforms were enacted.

King Hezekiah (716–687 B.C.) tried to reform the life of the nation but the attempt foundered. Things went from bad to worse under the reign of Manasseh (687–642 B.C.) and Amon (642–640 B.C.). Then a young king, Josiah, took over the reigns of government in 640 B.C. He had the sympathy of the people, and he was determined to pick up the urgent work of reform that had been neglected. At this time international tension had abated with the decline of Assyria. Thus a broad-based movement for national reform came into being, supported by government figures, the clergy, the prophets, and much of the population. It sought to implement the real constitution of the nation: the law of God. A new edition of that law, elaborated in what is now the book of Deuteronomy, had been composed around this time, having allegedly been "found" in the Temple.

During this period of general reform, someone had a clever idea. He decided to take advantage of all the popular traditions that had come down from the past in order to abet the reform movement. His basic theme was this: If someone reforms the life of the nation or paves the way for such reform, that person paves the way for a better future and helps to ensure its arrival. He was of the opinion that the general situation of moral and physical decay derived precisely from the fact that the Hebrew people were neglecting to observe the rights and duties spelled out in God's law. The people had to realize that fact, and he wrote his book to help them do it. His work is the book of Judges, in which we find the story of Samson.

The biblical author took all the ancient traditions of the era of the Judges and arranged them within a fixed schema that embodied his fundamental message. (1) When the Hebrew people stopped following the law of God during the period of the Judges, they lost their freedom and were oppressed by some foreign power (Jgs 2:1–3, 11–15; 3:7–8, 12–14; 4:1–2; 6:1–2; 10:6–8; 13:1). (2) When the Hebrew people repented for their sins and reformed their national life, God always raised up some leader on whom the power of the Spirit was bestowed in order to liberate the nation (Jgs 3:9–10, 15; 4:3ff; 6:7ff; 10:10ff). (3) This repentance and charismatic leadership resulted in a period of peace and tranquility in which the Hebrew people enjoyed liberty (Jgs 3:11–30; 5:31; 8:28; 15:32). (4) When the Hebrew people once again abandoned the law of God, oppression returned and the same process was repeated.

That is how the biblical author saw the story of the Judges. The Judges were charismatic leaders raised up by God in response to the good will of the Hebrew people. It was God's consistent response to personal conversion and national reform. Thus the reader could be sure that such divine intervention was possible once again. The people simply had to pave the way for such intervention by adopting a thoroughgoing reform of their national life. Their God was the God of the Judges, and the power of God's Spirit would once again guarantee the success of their reform efforts. Thus the long-distant past of the Judges took on life for the writer's contemporaries. The point was simple: If we want things to change for the better, we must do what our forefathers did.

The Hebrew author inserted the already existing story of Samson into the general context of his book. To make it fit into the general perspective and objective of his own work, he added a brief introduction: "Once more the Israelites did what was wrong in the eyes of the Lord, and he delivered them into the hands of the Philistines for forty years" (Jgs 13:1). He also added a concluding sentence about Samson: "He had been judge over Israel for twenty years" (Jgs 16:31; see also Jgs 15:20). Thus an old story, without sacrificing any of its popular flavor, began to serve an important and useful function for the people of the writer's own day. It became a summons to them, challenging them to face their own situation with realistic faith and to pave the way for the manifestation of God's power. It raised a question in the reader's mind: "Who will be our Samson today? What leader deserves our support because the power of God is manifestly at work in him?" The biblical author clearly intended his readers to deduce that the young king Josiah was the man they were looking for.

Touchups to the Story

Some questions still remain, however. What about this story of Samson? Did it really happen? Is it true that God really approved of all that is recounted? Of what use are those questionable accounts of murder and love affairs? What really happened? Can we possibly know?

At this point two things should be mentioned. First of all, we are dealing here with popular or folk literature. Secondly, the stories arose in a very specific context, that is, in an age when the Hebrews were subject to the oppression of the Philistines.

Popular literature does not adhere to the rules of newspaper reporting. It is not interested in giving a photographic version of the facts. Such folk literature is very open to "added touches." Facts may be padded to suit the interests that hold sway at a given moment. Furthermore, since this particular literature arose in a context of oppression, it gave expression to the longings of the Hebrew people. They wanted to overthrow the Philistines and regain their freedom.

To give an example of the process at work, we can cite what might have happened during World War II. European Resistance fighters might have blown up some small bridge in a Nazi-occupied country. People would tell the story in hushed tones, so that the incident was bruited about. They would enjoy telling the story because it would relieve their tension and quicken their hopes. It would prove that there were forces at work for regaining the freedom that they all longed for. But as the story spread, the size of the bridge might grow to enormous dimensions and other phenomenal details might be added.

Something similar happened in ancient Israel. The Philistines overran the country and the Hebrew people suffered greatly. There were various heroes in its Resistance movement against the Philistines. One of them was a figure named Samson, who put his stamp on a whole epoch. He was a man of great strength and courage and brutal audacity. Somehow he managed to keep alive the hopes of the Hebrew people and to pave the way for David's eventual overthrow of the Philistines many years later. Samson gradually became a legend. His story was touched up as it passed from mouth to mouth. It is now no longer possible to know exactly what he really did, just as it might be hard to find out the actual size of that bridge that was blown up.

The story woven around the person of Samson did have a real basis in history, but it was not designed to be an informational narrative about what actually happened. It came from a different source and it had a different objective. It arose as a way to give expression and support to the hopes of the harried Hebrew people. It served as an escape valve, enabling the people to breathe a sigh of relief. The Hebrew people wanted to go on living their own lives and hoping for freedom. The story of Samson told them that it was possible to have hope and courage, to go on resisting the Philistines, because they had an even greater force on their side: the Spirit of God.

This concrete objective prompted them to add wondrous and miraculous details to the basic story. It is a patriotic rather than a historical narrative, designed to raise the consciousness of the Hebrew people, keep them alert, and make sure that they do not give in to accommodation with the Philistine conquerors.

The Story of Samson

Samson's birth (Jgs 13). The description makes it clear that this child will be great. His father's name is Manoah ("tranquil"). The mother is supposedly sterile (Jgs 13:2), yet she she gives birth to a boy child whose name means "fire." This suggests that God intervened in a special way. The story describes what happened as if Samson's birth had been foretold by an "angel of the Lord." This angel tells the mother that her child is to be consecrated wholly to God; thus she must observe certain rules (Jgs 13:4). The child himself is never to cut his hair (Jgs 13:5). Already, then, the reader can glimpse something of Samson's destiny and also the origin of his strength. It is rooted in his total dedication to God, which opened the way for the manifestation of the Spirit. In the Bible, prior annunciation of a birth is part of a general framework which tells the reader that the child to be born has a very special mission in the carrying out of God's plan. Such is the case with Jacob (Gn 25:21–26), Samuel (1 Sm 1:1–28), John the Baptist (Lk 1:5–25), and Jesus Christ (Lk 1:26–37).

Samson's marriage (Jgs 14). Samson was a nonconformist. He had a hankering for a Philistine woman, one of his people's enemies, and he decided to marry her. No one could dissuade him from that course (Jgs 14:1–3). Later on the Hebrew people saw the hand of God in this, mysteriously arranging everything for their benefit. It was Samson's betrothal to a Philistine woman that served as the occasion for the victorious struggle against the Philistine rulers (Jgs 14:4). In other words, God writes straight with crooked lines, and God's ways are not our ways. Verses 5–20 of this chapter are clearly a legendary accretion to some fact that we cannot pinpoint precisely. Samson slays a lion but does not tell his parents. He proposes a riddle during his wedding feast, but he loses the wager because his wife keeps pestering him for the answer and tells her countrymen when she gets it. Samson then has to pay up with thirty lengths of linen and thirty changes of clothing. He goes out and kills thirty Philistine men to get the clothing. The Bible says that "the spirit of the Lord suddenly seized him" (Jgs 14:19) just before he set out for this mur-

derous work. Then Samson returns to his father's
house and Samson's wife is given in marriage to the
one who had been his best man.

Combat with the Philistines (Jgs 15). When Samson
went to see his wife sometime later, he learned that
his father-in-law had betrayed him by giving his
wife to another man. In a rage he went out and
grabbed three hundred foxes, tied their tails together two by two, fastened torches to each pair of
tails, and then set the foxes loose in the cornfields of
the Philistines. All their cultivated land was burned
up (Jgs 15:4–5). The Philistines took revenge by
burning Samson's wife and her father. Samson
struck back by killing many Philistines in "a great
slaughter," and then hid out in a cave (Jgs 15:6–8).
The Philistines followed with a general attack on
Samson's countrymen, much to their puzzlement
and dismay. Fearing worse problems, they sent out
a posse of three thousand men to seize Samson and
turn him over to the Philistines. Samson permitted
his capture and surrender to the Philistines. But just
as he was being handed over, the "spirit of the Lord
suddenly seized him." He burst his bonds, picked
up the jawbone of an ass, and slew a thousand men.
Weary and thirsty after this exploit, he asked God
for water. God split open a huge rock and water
flowed out of it. He rewarded the slaughter of a
thousand men with a miracle!

A tragic yet glorious end (Jgs 16). Samson went to

Gaza, a Philistine city, and entered a house of prostitution. The Philistines, hoping to entrap him, locked the city gates. But Samson merely ripped up the locked doors of the city gate and the gateposts and carted them off with him to the top of a hill east of Hebron—a considerable distance from the city (Jgs 16:1–3). Then Samson developed a passion for another Philistine woman named Delilah. The Philistines worked up another plot against Samson in which Delilah would play the key role. She was to find out the secret of Samson's strength. Three times Samson led her astray with his answer, but the fourth time he revealed to her that the secret of his strength lay in his seven enormous locks of hair which had never been cut. They were a mark of his consecration to God. The Philistines cut his hair while he was asleep, and so he did not have the strength to resist them when they came to capture him. They gouged out his eyes and imprisoned him.

The underlying lesson is that when we allow a third party to interfere between us and God, when we stray from God, we lose our strength and courage and become the hapless prey of human malice.

The Philistines had planned a great festival in honor of their God, Dagon. In the meantime Samson's hair had been growing back and his strength returning. In the midst of the festival Samson brings down the Philistine temple, killing himself and more Philistines than he had slain during his entire lifetime (Jgs 16:30).

The Point of the Story

The reader of these episodes cannot help but feel both repulsion and admiration: repulsion for the crimes which Samson committed and which the Bible does not cover up; admiration for Samson's boldness and authenticity. Samson is sincere, forthright, and completely free. He challenges convention and does not lie. He will not tolerate duplicity and so even slays his own countrymen when they try to serve the interests of the Philistines.

The Bible does not approve of Samson's crimes and weaknesses. It simply recounts the popular legend about him and indicates the way that led from oppression to liberty. Moreover, it consistently stresses the qualities that mark that journey from start to finish: sincerity and love of freedom. Thus it provides a clear bit of warning and advice for the reader: do not be led astray by the talk of a frivolous woman, for that can lead to chaos. It can even bring down a strong man like Samson.

These are popular stories, stories of a grateful people who are not unaware of misdeeds but who also know how to forgive. Samson was an outlaw, but he also incarnated a sacred ideal of the Hebrew people: love for liberty. He helped to bring about

the full recovery of Hebrew freedom in the age of
David. Looking back to the era of Samson from a
later age, the Hebrews saw the hand of God at work
in that strange story, and realized that God works
in strange ways.

There is much folklore in the story of Samson and
Delilah, but that does not diminish its value. There
is something more to the story than merely colorful
folklore, and that is why the Hebrew people were
deeply interested in it: It expresses the hope of the
Hebrew people in a better future, thanks to God's
help. It expresses their love of freedom and sincerity. It expresses their firm faith that God is with his
people in all circumstances. It expresses disap-
proval of those who choose accommodation, trying to get rid of the one who is truly free.

Further Conclusions

The Samson story gives a glimpse into the way
the Bible came into being and was shaped. It did not
happen in a day. The process was a slow one,
paralleling the gradual growth in awareness of the
Hebrew people. With the help and enlightenment
of God, they gradually came to an awareness of
their responsibilities.

So we find that in the Bible, and even within a
given book of the Bible, there are different layers of
thought coming from different epochs. The story of
Samson, for example, is presented from two differ-

ent viewpoints: the viewpoint of the writer living in
the time of King Josiah, and the viewpoint of the
Hebrew people who lived under Philistine domination for hundreds of years. Thus the book of Judges
seems to be a new building made out of old bricks.
When we study it, we realize that the aim of the
Bible is not simply to preserve the old stories and
traditions for their own sake, but rather to preserve
them in such a way that they might offer readers a
concrete, faith-imbued view of their own situation.
The aim of the Bible is to keep the Hebrew people
alert and awake, fully conscious of their responsibilities.

The story of Samson also reveals the honesty of
the Hebrew people in presenting their past history.
They do not cover up or hide anything. Without
approving of errors that may have been committed,
they try to perceive the good contained in them. It is
for this reason that the Bible is meaningful even
today. One need only take a cursory look at human
history to realize that all human activity is an ambivalent mixture of good and evil. Sometimes a
deed looks good on the surface but is evil at the
root. Jesus condemned this kind of acting as
pharisaical, because surface appearance did not reflect the inner person. Sometimes a deed looks evil
on the surface, but is basically good at the root. This
latter kind of deed pleases God much more than the
former. Jesus himself welcomes sinners, publicans,
and prostitutes.

Samson was a man who seemed to display much surface wickedness. But deep down there was something very good in him: sincerity, authenticity, and love of freedom. The history of the Church itself is a mixture of good and evil. Terrible things have been done in God's name, as the Crusades, the Inquisition, and the persecution of heterodox people clearly indicate. We have no right to condemn the attitudes of Samson, which force us to confront our own consciences. If we look at our own lives and deeds, we soon realize that there is a fine line between good and evil and that we are a mixture of both. But God does not leave us because of that. The Bible rips off our mask and confronts us with what we really are. Instead of covering up and justifying evil, it acknowledges and confesses it. It seeks to bring about reform and conversion.

The world does not like free human beings —people who do not follow the lead of the majority, who challenge and inconvenience everyone as Samson did. But very often it is people like Samson who effect a better future. Like Samson, those who are fighting for a better future today have their bad points and make many mistakes. But if we fail to recognize and acknowledge in such people the positive element and the summons of God, we may well be guilty of what Jesus called "the sin against the Holy Spirit." Jesus himself was accused of being possessed by a devil because he inconvenienced many people and because he took away their peace of mind. To justify themselves, they said that the enemy of God was responsible for the things that God was doing for human freedom in and through Jesus Christ (Mk 3:23–30). This sin against the Holy Spirit cannot be pardoned because it blocks up the well from which we draw water to purify the evil in our lives.

5

The Prophets: Where Is the God We Believe In?

Questions about the Prophets

How does a prophet know that God has commanded him to say a certain thing? How does the vocation of the prophet arise? How can one distinguish between a true prophet and a false prophet, since both claim to speak in God's name? What is the prophet's mission? How does he operate? What does he teach us about God? Do prophets exist today? These are some of the questions that crop up in our minds as we read the prophetical books of the Bible.

In the Old Testament sixteen books are attributed to prophets. Four of them are considered to be books of "major" prophets: Isaiah, Jeremiah (together with Lamentations and Baruch), Ezechiel, and Daniel. The twelve other prophetical books are considered to belong to "minor" prophets: Hosea,

Joel, Amos, Obadiah, Jonah, Micah, Nahum, Habakkuk, Zephaniah, Haggai, Zechariah, and Malachi. The division into "major" and "minor" is based on the quantity of material that the prophet has left behind for us. There are other prophets in the Bible of whom we possess no written record, e.g., Elijah and Elisha.

Many of these men are little more than names to us. It is now impossible for us to know who they were, how they lived, and exactly what they did. But critical study of their writings and a knowledge of both biblical and secular history does enable us to get a fair picture of the complicated human situation in which they were obliged to live and to carry out their mission.

The words "prophet" and "prophecy" evoke connotations of "foretelling the future" in our minds. In reality the root word (Gr. *pro-fémi*) means "to speak in the name of" someone. The prophets are people who speak in the name of God, and who *know* they are speaking in God's name.

The Prophet's Vocation

It is difficult to get inside the innermost depths of another person, to lift the veil of mystery that surrounds that person's life with God. The vocation of the prophet is framed within this sphere of impenetrable mystery. But if we ponder some of the hints that the prophets themselves have left us in their writings, we can form some idea of how the prophetic vocation comes into being. Let us look at two examples.

The prophet Amos was a plain man of the people, a common laborer and herdsman (Am 7:14). He lived in a period of economic progress that had been stimulated by King Jeroboam (783–743 B.C.) of the Northern Kingdom. Unfortunately that economic progress was grounded on the collective egotism of selfish classes and social groups. Self-interest led to unjust social divisions and the oppression of large sectors of the general population (Am 5:7; 2:6–7; 3:10). The Hebrew people, whom God had liberated earlier, had become enslaved once again—this time to their fellow Hebrews.

Amos's life was deeply enmeshed in the life of the Hebrew people. His faith and his good sense told him that such a state of affairs was contrary to the will of God. It was a paradoxical situation that gradually turned into a serious problem for Amos; he could not get his mind off it. Everything reminded him of the injustice in the nation, and he could not help but foresee the divine punishment that it would eventually provoke. A raging fire in the woods reminded him that God was going to consume and burn away all the existing injustices (Am 7:4–6), and a basket of ripe fruit reminded him that Israel was ripe for God's punishment (Am 8:1–3). Facts and events began to speak for themselves, turning into a summons and an appeal. Gradually Amos became more and more aware of the situation, finally deciding that God wanted him to speak out: "The lion has roared; who is not terrified? The Lord God has spoken; who will not prophesy?" (Am 3:8) He dropped everything and began prophesying without mincing his words (Am 7:10–17).

The story of Hosea begins with these words: "This is the beginning of the Lord's message by Hosea. He said, Go, take a wanton for your wife and get children of her wantonness" (Hos 1:2). The most likely explanation is this. Hosea married some woman who, though happily married, eventually left him and became a prostitute. But Hosea continued to love her, and his faithful and unselfish love made the woman realize what a worthwhile man he was; so she came back to him. In this way Hosea discovered that he himself was an example and a dispenser of the regenerating force of love. Living within the Hebrew people, he came to see that this personal experience—both painful and fruitful—had much broader significance. The Hebrew nation was abandoning its spouse, God, and prostituting itself with the worship of other deities. But just as he had continued to love his unfaithful wife, so God continued to have a faithful and unselfish love for his people. God's love could regenerate the people and bring them back to being his faithful spouse and nation.

Hosea gradually became aware of his mission. He would remind the Hebrew people about the unrequited love of God, thus hoping to prompt them to conversion. His prophecies are forceful and violent precisely because jealousy is one of the most violent emotions that can exist in a human being.

These two examples show us that the prophet was a person in whom the conscious awareness of the people of God culminated in the conscious awareness of an individual person. The prophet perceives the call of God in and through his own personal situation in the midst of the Hebrew people. His clear-cut perception of God's demands leads him to see with equal clarity what the life of the people should really be. He is at once a "man of God" and a "man of the people." He deeply feels his involvement with God and with his people, and he realizes that he cannot keep silent any longer. He speaks with authority because his words find their source in God and in the age-old consciousness and tradition of his people. His vocation is born of a confrontation between the real and the ideal.

Severe punishments are reserved for people who claim to be speaking in God's name when in fact they have not been sent by God (Dt 18:20). To prove the authencity of his mission, the prophet foretells the future. His prophecies are short-range ones, and their fulfillment proves that God is with him (Dt 18:21–22; Jer 28:9; Ez 33:33). In this way the false prophet is distinguished from the true one.

Mission of the Prophets

The mission and activity of the prophet is always conditioned by the actual situation of the people to whom he is addressing his message. The prophet is an instrument in God's hands. He is to help the people to keep moving toward the objective to which they committed themselves through their covenant with God. The prophet, if you will, is the man sent to collect the pledge that the nation freely made with God and itself.

Because of the Exodus event, the group of people who left Egypt consciously realized that they were the "people of God," and that with God they were responsible for carrying out a project of liberation. This awareness was the dynamic force that kept the group journeying on without ever coming to a definitive stop. They were opening a way to the future guaranteed by God's fidelity and power. This fundamental attitude entailed faith, courage, hope, self-giving, and love. It was rooted in their experience and in their unshakeable conviction that God was with them, that God was summoning them at every moment, and that they had a mutual commitment with God.

This experiential awareness of friendship with God, also called the "covenant," was structured into certain attitudes and behavior patterns. There was the law, cultic worship, various institutions, feasts, celebrations, and customary practices such as pilgrimages to the Temple. Various traditions kept the past alive and transmitted it to future generations. There were also images and representative items, such as the ark of the covenant and the golden calf. There were institutions like prophecies, the priesthood, and the monarchy, and popular practices such as prayers and wisdom literature. The intense life of the nation coursed through all these, keeping alive in each succeeding generation the awareness that they were the people of God and must remain faithful to God.

All these structures and behavior patterns had arisen out of the Hebrew people's particular faith in God. They were tools designed to keep alive their faith, hope, and generosity. They were means to an end, not ends in themselves, and they were given direction and critical examination on the basis of that end. At some point a given behavior pattern might no longer give real expression to the people's authentic way of life. For one reason or another, it might no longer convey or transmit the value that it had been designed to transmit. At that point the pattern would be criticized, and then emended or eliminated. Once again the governing criterion was the original plan God had in mind and for which he had fashioned his people.

These structures and behavior patterns were human creations designed to give expression to the faith of the people. But the great problem with humankind has always been its understandable and inveterate desire for individual and national security. After much searching, people would develop a way of living that expressed their deepest convictions. They would come to regard this as a great achievement and look to it for assurance and security. A phenomenon thus takes place among the Hebrew people: The forms of life that had allowed them to express their friendship with God ceased to embody or promote a continuing search for a better future. Instead they would come to embody the inveterate search for security. Losing contact with their original source—an awareness that they were the people of God—the forms would cease to be channels of authentic living. The inner vitality of the nation would diminish considerably, but the external structure or behavior pattern would continue as before as if nothing had changed. The skeletal framework might look healthy, but there was no authentic life within.

Some people wanted to cling to those external structures and patterns. They would come to regard them as admission tickets entitling them to intimacy with God and divine assistance. But the structures and patterns would now be nothing more than social conventions, empty shells that let people entertain the illusion that all is well with God when in fact there is no interior life. Fragile by their very nature, these social conventions would be defended by close-minded, violent attacks on anyone who chose to criticize them.

It is here that the prophets went into action. Their mission and activity was almost always prompted by this short-circuit between interior life and externalized behavior. They would denounce the false sense of security behind which the people were hiding—often unwittingly. They would unsettle the people and push them in search of new behavior patterns that would give renewed expression and stimulus to faith and life. They would condemn the external forms which kept the people immobile. The most immediate reaction of the people was a feeling of insecurity. They felt they were being deprived of something that had provided them with peace of mind and a sense of tranquility.

The prophet always acts in God's name. He tries to show people that their conception of God, as it is embodied in their external structures and behavior patterns, is not a conception of the true God revealed to their forefathers in the desert after they had been liberated from Egypt. The prophets themselves have this clear-cut vision because they are men of God; hence they are in a position to denounce the people's errors. They do not simply teach the people *about* God. They reveal God in their own attitudes, showing the Hebrew people that God is always different from, and greater than, anything they had imagined. God does not permit himself to be domesticated by human beings. No human form, however religious it may be, can contain God. Let us consider briefly what this means in concrete terms.

Prophetic Criticism of the People's Conception of God

The golden calf. After the Hebrew people had escaped Egypt, they fashioned an image of a golden calf. It was meant to give concrete embodiment to the force with which God had freed them (Ex 32:4). But that image entailed a serious danger. It became possible for the people to equate God with the many other deities who were represented under the likeness of a bull or calf. It was possible to go overboard in visualizing and localizing the power of God, which cannot be confined or limited to any one image or instrument. Much later Jeroboam reintroduced the image of the golden calf (1 Kgs 12:28) to give a religious cast to the political revolution he had accomplished. It became a source of apostasy, condemned in the Bible in the most vehement terms. A golden calf is not suitable for expressing faith in God (1 Kgs 12:31–13:2).

The high places. Once the Hebrew people had entered the promised land, they began to worship God in the "high places," under every spreading tree. They felt that the power of God was concentrated in such places, because God's power managed to raise up huge trees in desert soil. Solomon, for example, went to worship God at Gibeon, "the chief hill-shrine" (1 Kgs 3:4). But there was a danger in this form of worship. Once again God might come to be identified with the many other deities who were worshipped in the same way and in the same places. Once again the action of God might become too localized, and the locale of human encounter with God restricted. When this potential danger became real, the prophets rose up to condemn this form of worship in vehement terms. More than one prophet likened it to prostitution (see Jer 3:1–2:7; Is 1:29–31; Hos 2:6–7). Instead of giving expression and impetus to the people's friendship with God, worship in the high places was undermining the life of the people and the nation. It had to be criticized and condemned.

King and monarchy. God had promised that the Hebrews would be his people and that he would be their God. With the passage of time, this promise was incarnated and individualized in the person of the king: "I will be his father, and he shall be my son" (2 Sm 7:14). Thus the king became the visible sign of God's friendship with the Hebrew people, the instrument that would ensure that God's will prevailed. Gradually, however, the presence of a king in their midst became an excuse for feeling comfortable and oversecure. Since the king was in their midst, the people felt that God was obliged to help them; after all, God himself had promised that there would always be a king on the throne of David

(1 Sm 7:16). Once again the prophets stepped in: The throne of David will become a dilapidated shack (Am 9:11), none of his descendants will occupy the kingly throne (Jer 22:30), and the king of Israel will disappear once and for all (Hos 10:15). The fact of having a king offers no guarantee of safe conduct to anyone.

The Temple. The Hebrew people encountered God in the Temple: "How dear is thy dwelling-place, thou Lord of Hosts! I pine, I faint with longing for the courts of the Lord's temple" (Ps 84:1–2). Pilgrimages, processions, psalms, canticles, and prayers—all these were bound up with the Temple, the dwelling-place of God. Possessing the Temple, the Hebrew people felt that God was surely with them and committed to their cause. They took good care of the Temple, and this preoccupation gradually caused them to forget the more serious obligation of living the faith in their daily lives. They overlooked the fact that the Temple was merely an embodiment of that faith. Hence Jeremiah launches a direct frontal attack on the Temple (Jer 7: 1–15), accusing the people of murder and lying and warning them that the Temple will not keep them safe. The Temple will be totally destroyed—as the shrine of Shiloh had been.

Cultic worship. Cult was the core of the nation's life. It recalled the past and rendered it present, enabling each succeeding generation to commit itself to God's plan and to take cognizance of its rights and duties. But worship was gradually reified into ritual, losing its connection with life. The people no longer lived out the presence of God in their daily actions. Worship became a service rendered for a stipulated period of time in return for God's protection. Great care was given to the ritual ceremonies, but not to one's everyday actions. The prophets called attention to the phoniness, asserting that such ritual was of no use whatsoever: "Your countless sacrifices, what are they to me? says the Lord. I am sated with whole-offerings of rams and the fat of buffaloes. . . . When you lift your hands outspread in prayer, I will hide my eyes from you. Though you offer countless prayers, I will not listen" (Is 1:11, 15). Worship *in itself* offers no guarantee of divine protection.

Jerusalem. The city of peace, Jerusalem is praised in numerous psalms as the symbol of God's power and operative presence in the life of the nation (Pss 122; 137; 147). It was the heart of the nation's life, the "holy mountain." But its glory would be of no real use because it had not inspired the people to practice justice. It would be totally destroyed just as any other city might be (Is 3:8–9). The mere fact that one lived in Jerusalem guaranteed nothing.

The promised land. Abraham set out on a journey toward the land that had been promised to him, but it was not conquered until much later by Joshua. The conquest of the land was a sign that God would fulfill his promises. Dwelling in that land, the Hebrew people were able to feel sure that God was with them. They took this certainty too much for granted, however, and lived as if they had reached the final goal of their journey. The prophets then stepped in to unmask this presumptuous attitude for the delusion that it was. The Hebrew people would be torn away from their land, driven into exile, and forced to see their land destroyed (Jer 13:15–19; 4:23–28).

The day of Yahweh. The Hebrews lived in the hope and expectation that some day God would come to manifest his justice. He would destroy the wicked and exalt his own people. It would be a day of light and peace and victory for them. Cherishing this illusion, they neglected everything else they were supposed to do. Then the prophets brought them shocking news about the day of Yahweh: "Fools who long for the day of the Lord, what will the day of the Lord mean to you? It will be darkness, not light. It will be as when a man runs from a lion, and a bear meets him, or turns into a house and leans his hand on the wall, and a snake bites him. The day of the Lord is indeed darkness, not light, a day of gloom with no dawn" (Am 5:18–20).

The chosen people. The Hebrew nation owed its origin to the fact that God had taken them out of Egypt and made a covenant with them. They were God's "chosen people" and this honorable designation was the motivating force behind their great quest. Gradually, however, it led the Hebrews into thinking they were privileged beings. They came to rely more on this privileged status than on the fidelity to God which it demanded of them. But Amos warned them: "Are not you Israelites like Cushites to me? says the Lord. Did I not bring Israel up from Egypt, the Philistines from Caphtor, the Aramaeans from Kir?" (Am 9:7). His point was that in God's eyes the Israelites were no better than other nations, no better in fact than two of their worst enemies, the Philistines and the Aramaeans. The mere fact of membership in God's chosen people did not guarantee security or favoritism.

Children of Abraham. Abraham was the great friend of God whose intercession could save whole towns (Gn 18:16–33). It was an honor to be able to say: "We are Abraham's descendants" (Jn 8:33). But many Hebrews relied on the designation without acting as Abraham had. John the Baptist, the last prophet of the Old Testament, makes it clear that the title alone avails little: "Prove your repentance by the fruits it bears; and do not begin saying to yourselves, 'We have Abraham for our father.' I tell you that God can make children for Abraham out of these stones here" (Jn 3:8). Another prop was pulled out from under the Hebrew people.

The law of God. God gave his people the law. Those who observe it will be safe and secure (Jer 8:8). Hence the people tried to explain the law clearly and to find out exactly what it demanded, so that they could secure salvation for themselves. But somehow the law turned into an instrument for coercing God. Saint Paul points out that both the Jews with the law and the Greeks without it are "all under the power of sin" (Rom 3:9). "No human being can be justified in the sight of God for having kept the law" (Rom 3:20).

The prophets undermined all the supports on which the Hebrew people had relied. They swept the floor clean and flashed the light of truth into every nook and cranny. All the supposedly sure lines of contact with God were cut. The prophets opened the ground under their feet and showed the people that there was no easy certainty on which they could rely. It was not that these supports were false in themselves. They were counterfeit because they had ceased to serve as a channel for God's summons in the movement towards the promised future. They were false because they had become tools for compromise and oppression in God's name.

Today a prophet might well say the same about what we regard as sacrosanct and inviolable. And again today the prophet would probably be scorned and rejected in the name of God. Jesus Christ himself was rejected in the name of God and tradition: "This fellow is no man of God; he does not keep the Sabbath" (Jn 9:16). No religious practice or work can *in itself* lay hold of and coerce God. If people cling self-assuredly to attendance at Mass or recitation of the rosary or vigil-light services, then they are relying on a purely personal projection of their own; it is not God but rather a nonexistent, mythical deity. It certainly is not the living and true God whom the prophets intimately knew and worshipped. There is no lever on earth that can move the heavens by itself. The prophets criticized all such ideas. They made it clear that people could not rely blindly on such forms under the delusion that they could thereby coerce God into helping them.

Thus it is easy to see why the prophets met with a great deal of resistance. They meddled with the most important props for ensuring personal security. We can readily appreciate what the author of the letter to the Hebrews has to say about the suffering and persecution of the prophets (Heb 11:32–38).

Seemingly very negative in tone, the criticism made by the prophets stemmed from their view of God. This view was in marked contrast with the structures and behavior patterns of the Hebrew people. The prophets would not permit people to become alienated from life, to flee into a separate religious world of rite, ceremony, and cult. Doing this empties those practices of any real meaning. If they were alive today, those prophets would be the first to say that such religion is truly the "opiate of the people." One need only read a few pages of their writings to be convinced of that.

Now we must turn to the positive side of the prophetic message and its radical criticism.

The Living and True God of the Prophets

Was everything wrong in the eyes of the prophets? Although the prophets did burn all the bridges that people had mistakenly assumed would lead them to God, they also fashioned a bridge of their own. This bridge was faith. It could establish real contact with God, and it could offer a guarantee of God's presence.

In a deep and thorough way the prophets lived the presence of God. They were men of God. God surpasses everyone and everything. God cannot be grabbed or lassoed; God cannot be turned into a beast of burden and loaded down with the weight of human yearnings and desires. God cannot be tamed or domesticated. Instead of serving God, we want God to serve us; and so we employ ritual and worship as sacralized magic. But in so doing we are turning things upside down.

For the prophets, God was a wholly *gratuitous* presence offering friendship to whomever chose to accept it. But God wants respect in this relationship of friendship. If someone offers his friendship, God wants the other party to have confidence in him. God does not want the other party to use devious and spurious tactics in order to guarantee the benefits of that friendship. That would indicate a lack of confidence, and it would be reason enough to withhold one's friendship from the other party in the future. If we approach a friend for help and support, we do not point to the presents and favors our friend has offered us in the past. We simply appeal to the tie of friendship. We tell him what we plan to do and ask for his help as a friend. Our appeal is based on the tie of friendship and the mutual commitment it entails.

God made a commitment with human beings and offered them his friendship. He wants the tie of friendship to be respected in his case also. He demands faith and confidence as the initial preconditions for any further understanding. God's presence in our midst is a guaranteed certainty because God himself has said so. At the same time, however, God is strong enough to evade any improper approach to him where faith and confidence are lacking: e.g., the golden calf, the high places, the monarchy, Jerusalem, the Temple, cultic worship, and so forth. All these, from ancient ritual to modern-day procession, are relative. They do not have guaranteed purchasing power in themselves. When it reaches the point where we try to use any one of them to buy our way into heaven, they merit critical denunciation and condemnation from the prophets of today.

These various approaches are of no guaranteed value in themselves. They can be good, useful, and even necessary when they are used as tools to express our faith and confidence—which are required conditions for any real contact with God. But the tools are merely signposts pointing us toward God. God remains *far beyond* anything and everything we might imagine, and at the same time *much closer* to us in friendship than any exterior expression. These expressions are like telephone lines. They are a means of communication, yet they do not compel anyone to pick up the receiver at the other end. The party at the other end of the line can take the phone off the hook and leave me talking to myself. But if those instruments are indeed expressions of my faith, then they do make contact with God who does not break off the connection. In the name of his own fidelity and loyalty, God will stay in contact with us, lending his aid and support.

On the surface it would seem that the prophets thrust human beings into a state of total insecurity and uncertainty. In reality they lay the basis for the most solid security a human being can possess: the absolute certainty that God is there. He is not far away, he is with us. His name is Emmanuel, "God with us." And he is a loyal, friendly, powerful God. At the same time, however, he transcends us. He is always the Other, and we cannot domesticate him. His relationship with us is sovereign and free, so that he can evade any attempt to dominate him. The attitude of God, who is both close to us and far away, is a challenge and an accusation. It reminds us that there is at least *one* who manages to evade our grasping clutches. It also entails a criticism of the domination which one human being exercises over another, awakens the dominated party to the true nature of the relationship, and prompts a desire to have human dignity respected.

Thus the attitude God adopts towards us is one which helps us to adopt the same attitude towards others. The only real and effective means for linking another person to ourselves is faith, trust, and disinterested love. When a human being is wise enough to take a proper stance before God, then God in fact does feel obliged to help him. As one Psalm puts it: "Because his love is set on me, I will deliver him" (Ps 91:14). God feels obliged to help because such a person takes God seriously. This is not easy, however, because we must leap into the dark, adopt an attitude of faith and confidence in the words of the other party. In sum, it is an attitude which allows the Other to be Other, which allows God to be God.

This is precisely what the prophets have to tell us about God. It is all summed up in the name that God chose for himself: Yahweh, that is, "I will be present." God tells Moses: "I AM; that is who I am" (Ex 3:14). In other words, God will certainly be present to help Moses and his people; but God will decide *when* and *where* and *how* to display this salvific presence. We can count on God, but we cannot coerce God. The very name of God is a summons to faith, and God gives proof of his liberating presence. The first great proof was the Exodus from Egypt. The last and ultimate proof was the coming of Jesus Christ, who is Emmanuel; and this proof is still in process (Mt 1:23).

God, perceived in these terms and so incorporated into life, is the core and source of all prophetic activity. At the same time God provides us with a new vision of life itself. That is why the prophets never lose hope, even when they are enmeshed in the trials and tribulations which they themselves may have foretold. However much he criticizes, the message of the prophet is one of hope. The criticism is necessary when some way of living threatens to narrow and harden life so badly that it will stifle this hope in the people, particularly in the hearts of the poor and lowly.

Today's Prophets

Prophets usually do not use professional titles. They do not print their mission on a business card. Today the prophetic movement in the Church and the world is quite strong. Criticism of obsolete structures and behavior patterns is underway, triggered by Vatican II itself. In the days of ancient Israel the prophetic movement was a cultural as well as a faith-inspired movement within the chosen people. The same is true today. Prophecy is a cultural datum which, within the Church, takes on a specific faith-inspired dimension. Christians are not the only ones who are criticizing obsolete structures and behavior patterns. They are part of the overall movement, taking their own particular cue from their faith in God.

Today there are people within the Church who are trying to overcome the alienation in which many Christians live out their lives, lost in the grip of practices that no longer serve to express friendship with God, but merely the search for human security. The rigid maintenance of the existing situation, both inside the Church and in society at large, is not due to the common people alone; it is also due to those in authority. Thus the criticism of the prophets today is also directed against those in power, even as it was in the days of ancient Israel. That is what Jesus Christ himself did. He criticized the Pharisees and other religious leaders. For the common people he had compassion, since he saw them as sheep without a shepherd.

Clearly, then, the mission of the prophet is a hazardous one. When one becomes aware of such a mission, as Amos and Hosea did, the feeling is not a pleasant one. One thinks twice about it. Like Moses (Ex 3:11–4:13) and Jeremiah (Jer 1:6), today's prophet can find good reasons and pretexts for escaping such a difficult task. But prophets will continue to raise their voices today even as they did long ago, however much others may advise them against it: "The lion has roared; who is not terrified? The Lord God has spoken; who will not prophesy?" (Am 3:8).

6

From Hezekiah to Josiah:
The History of a Reform

"The high priest Hilkiah told Shaphan the adjutant-general that he had discovered the book of the law in the house of the Lord . . . " (2 Kgs 22:8). That piece of information was like a stone dropped into a calm lake. Soon the ripples were spreading out over the whole surface of the nation's life. There are historical situations in which many factors converge suddenly at a given point that could not have been foreseen. The air is heavy with expectation, but no one knows exactly what is going to happen. When it does happen, it is as if some powerful generator had just been switched on to send a current of light through the dark night. All the lights go on because the cables have gradually been laid over the course of time. People have been waiting in the dark, preparing for the event, but its occurrence is still a surprise. Then suddenly everything seems changed.

That is precisely what happened when Hilkiah

reported his discovery. It was the eighteenth year in the reign of King Josiah, the year 622 B.C. (2 Kgs 22:3). We do not know much about the historical circumstances surrounding the discovery of the law in the Temple, nor do we know exactly how the book of the law came to find its way there. But we do know something about the movement that was intertwined with discovery, and that is what interests us here.

Historical movements, like huge trees whose roots are buried in the soil of preceding centuries, are irreversible in their growth pattern. Nothing can stop them. They grow stronger than the individuals involved with them. At the same time, however, individuals can exert an influence on them for good or ill. Because of their influence, it may happen that the power unleashed at a given moment is too great. The result may be that things become worse than they were before. That is exactly what happened with the reform we are considering here.

The Roots of Reform

In 722 B.C., a hundred years before the discovery of the law, a great catastrophe befell Israel, the Northern Kingdom of Palestine. Earlier it had split from the Southern Kingdom, now called Judah. In 722 B.C. Shalmaneser, the king of Assyria, invaded the Northern Kingdom. Assyria was the great world power of the time, and its army destroyed the capital of the Northern Kingdom (Samaria), devastated the land, deported the native population, and resettled people from other countries in the land of Israel (2 Kgs 17). The smoldering fires of revolt and subversion were thus stamped out, and the history of the Northern Kingdom came to a close (2 Kgs 17:18). But the warfare continued. The Assyrian armies moved southward, skirted the hilly kingdom of Judah, and continued on to meet the armies of Egypt in the Gaza Strip.

The destruction of Samaria was a dire warning to the small kingdom of Judah, which lay isolated in the highlands as the two great powers engaged in battle. The Hebrew people of the Northern Kingdom had ceased to exist as an independent entity because they had abandoned the unifying center of Hebrew national life. They had ceased to be faithful to the covenant and law of God, which was the true constitution of the nation (2 Kgs 17:7–18; 18:21). But the same infidelity, the same cancerous disintegration, existed in Judah (2 Kgs 17:19). Its escape from invasion was due more to luck than to merit. It had been spared because shortly before this, Ahaz, the king of Judah, had gotten on friendly terms with Assyria (2 Kgs 16:5–6; 7–18). He chose not to enter an alliance with the Northern Kingdom against Assyria, and even went so far as to ask Assyria for aid against the Northern Kingdom and to pay tribute to the Assyrian ruler.

What position should Judah take now? Should it side with Assyria? No, because that would negate a whole past effort of struggle and faith. Even when it was helping others, Assyria was really looking out for its own interests. It wanted to ensure its own security and domination of the world. The Assyrian threat from outside continued to grow, while inside Judah's resistance withered away. Ahaz was an impotent leader; he did not know how to tackle the critical situation. The prophet Isaiah had already tried to rekindle the king's faith in the future that God had in mind for his people (Is 7:1–25), but his words found no echo in the mediocre ruler. In his desperation Ahaz had even gone so far as to immolate his own son in order to win the protection of alien deities (2 Kgs 16:3). There was no fight left in him, no feeling of hope, no strength to resist. The people had lost any reason for living, and the inner void widened each day. Isaiah had been right when he said: "Have firm faith, or you will not stand firm" (Is 7:9). But how was such faith to be reenkindled in the people?

Ahaz died. Hezekiah, a youthful but capable political leader, took over the reigns of government at the age of twenty-five and ruled for almost thirty years. He was a man of faith who "put his trust in the Lord" (2 Kgs 18:5). He had confidence in the future that God had in mind, and he tried to communicate this faith to others. Thus he sparked a yearning for reform that he tried to articulate and implement. A breath of new life stirred in the nation

and gave new enthusiasm to everyone. Apathy
faded away, and the void was filled. A new mentality began to take shape among the people. New
ideas arose concerning God, worship, and both the
past and future of the nation. So far they were just
ideas, but they were forceful and ardent ideas that
took wings and began to flutter through people's
minds. These new ideas and the reform movement
sparked by Hezekiah lay behind the book of the law
that Hilkiah would discover in the temple a
hundred years later.

First Steps

The reform movement took shape and began to
exert an influence on every sector of the nation's
life. The faith was purified, the sources of magic
and superstition were rooted out (2 Kgs 18:3–4; 2
Chr 29:3–11). Injustices were eliminated, and the
law of God was solemnly reinstated as the true
constitution of the nation (2 Chr 30:1–27). Age-old
traditions were collected and anthologized (Prv
25:1). Jerusalem was restored, and its defenses
were refurbished for any eventuality (2 Chr 32:1–5).
Hezekiah made provisions for ensuring a good
supply of water in the event of siege. The reservoir
and conduit system engineered by him still im-
presses sightseers today (2 Kgs 20:20). He also
gained victory over a traditional enemy, the Philistines (2 Kgs 18:8), purified the temple (2 Chr

19:12–17), and reformed both the priesthood and the cultic worship of the nation (2 Chr 31:1–21).

A new nation was rising out of the ashes of despair and degradation. Hezekiah had somehow managed to touch a vital nerve and restore hope in a dispirited people. The crucial axis of this reform was the spiritual and religious renewal of the people. They made an abrupt turn and went back to the ruling center of their life as a nation: their living covenant with God. Their remembrance of their own past as a nation took on new vitality and vividness (2 Chr 30:5–9, 13–20). New hope and a clear desire to live and fight bravely came into being, grounded in a new-found sense of faith.

Hezekiah managed to reopen the door to the future when it seemed to be on the point of closing for good. He did this primarily through his reform of the liturgy, which embodies the authentic expression of the nation's life. He thus provided access to the vital forces at the heart of the nation's life, so that the Hebrew people were able to rediscover their true identity as the people of God. That was his great merit, and it would go down to his credit in Hebrew history: "There was nobody like him among all the kings of Judah who succeeded him or among those who had gone before him" (2 Kgs 18:5).

His activity was not confined to the internal affairs of his country, however. As a good political leader, he kept his eye on the far horizons of international politics. A tiny nation such as Judah could not close itself off in isolated nationalism. The Egyptian pharaoh had managed to recover from the earlier defeat and consolidate Egypt's position on the international scene. The balance of power, which had been upset by Assyria's victorious advance, was now restored. Once again an anti-Assyrian movement began to take shape, fomented and fed by Egypt. The pro-Egyptian faction grew stronger in the government of Hezekiah, seeking to win him over to its outlook. At the same time the prophet Isaiah, who counselled Hezekiah in religious and political matters, stuck to his previous outlook. He had earlier advised Ahaz not to look to Egypt for support, and he told Hezekiah the same thing. Egypt was not to be trusted (Is 30:1–7; 31:1–3). But Hezekiah did not listen to this advice, choosing instead to take an active part in the international power play (2 Kgs 18:21).

Assyria did not sit on the sidelines long. It soon stepped in and crushed the opposition movement. Judah was invaded, its towns taken one by one (2 Kgs 18:13). The only town that remained free was Jerusalem, whose defensive fortifications had been carefully shored up by Hezekiah over a period of years. We do not really know why, but Jerusalem did hold out and was not taken by the Assyrian forces or even frontally assaulted. Hezekiah came out a winner.

As is always the case in war, each contending party has its own version of what happened. The Hebrew version in the Bible says that Sennacherib laid siege to the city with an army of four hundred thousand men and caused great panic; but then an angel of the Lord stepped in, decimated his army, and forced him to retreat (2 Kgs 18:13–19:37; 2 Chr 32:9–23). The Assyrian version of the same event, found in the city of Nineveh by archeologists, gives a different reason. Whatever the case may be, the retreat of Sennacherib aroused great euphoria among the inhabitants of Jerusalem, and the event went to Hezekiah's head. He plunged headlong into the international political conspiracy against Assyria (2 Kgs 20:12–19). The people felt greater confidence in themselves and their own strength; they could hardly contain their gratitude (2 Chr 32:23). This event and its outcome helped to advance the internal renewal of the country.

Opposition Forces in Control

The winds of fortune can change direction, however. Hezekiah's successor, his son Manasseh, was a disappointment to the people and a failure as a ruler. An incompetent man, he did nothing to carry through the reform movement that had been started with so much good will and hope. A devotee of political intrigue, he had no time for religion or justice. Everything began to regress, and the backward movement lasted for fifty years or more. Manasseh began to rule around the age of twelve, and he was still in power when he died at the age of sixty-seven (2 Kgs 21:1–16). Nevertheless, the people retained an awareness that change was necessary, and they felt a nostalgic longing for the earlier spirit of reform.

Political intrigue took control of government affairs, and there was little interest in the law of God or the plight of the people (2 Kgs 21:16). Events took a predictable course. Amon, the successor of Manasseh, was assassinated (2 Kgs 21:33) because a group of military leaders and government officials wanted a ruler who would look after their special interests. The murder of the king, however, proved to be the last straw. Despite their disappointment with their recent kings, the common people still identified with the Davidic monarchy, and so they rose up in reaction. An assault on the king was an assault on the Hebrew people, and they rose up against the military men who had killed Amon and deposed them from power. The ringleaders were slain, and the reins of government were transferred to a legitimate descendant of David. He was eight years old at the time, and his name was Josiah (2 Kgs 22:1). From what we know, the running of the government was taken over by a priest named Hilkiah until the boy reached the age when he could govern in his own right. The year was 640 B.C.

Renewed Fervor for Reform

This violent turn of events stirred the awareness of the Hebrew people and gave them a new consciousness of their power. It was a new beginning.

They reversed the process of decline started with Manasseh. The desire to put through basic, thoroughgoing reforms reappeared in intensified form. And the pervading situation both inside and outside the country helped to foster this desire.

On the international front, Assyria was governed by Assurbanipal. He brought peace to the international scene, but it was the peace of the grave. His cruel policies and murderous aggression silenced those who were his enemies. Thousands were murdered or deported or tortured or struck down in some other way. In the later years of his reign he was able to relax his vigilance somewhat and devote himself to study and pleasure-seeking. He left behind a huge, recently uncovered library, and high-relief hunting scenes of astonishing beauty. His reign marked the high point of Assyrian power, and decline would soon set in. Egypt did not yet represent a real threat, but it was again beginning to revolt. Babylon, the third major world power, had not yet grown into a real threat and was viewed sympathetically by the nations that had been oppressed by Assyria. Even Hezekiah had held secret discussions with an envoy from Babylon (2 Kgs 20:12–15).

On the home front in Judah, a nationalist movement began to grow. The elimination of Amon's murderers meant that most people took sides with the new king even though he was still a youth. He was, after all, the ruler whom they had brought to power. Around this time there also appeared two prophets who summoned the people to reform and purification: Jeremiah and Zephaniah. The reform movement widened and took real hold of the country. It had the support of most people, and the international situation made it feasible.

The march forward began, led by the king. But as yet no one knew exactly what road to take. Something was still missing, and eighteen years went by before the reform movement would find the solid roots it needed (2 Kgs 22:3). It does seem, however, that some groping initiatives were taken during that early period (2 Chr 34:3–7). The cable lines, as it were, had been installed, but as yet no electric generator had been found. The nation had to wait until Hilkiah made his great discovery in the Temple. Then the road ahead became clear to everyone, and the whole nation set out optimistically for the future.

History of the Reform Charter

The law found in the Temple was the age-old law of God in a newly revised and augmented edition that corresponded to the new age. The ideas that had been sparked by Hezekiah and then submerged in the reign of Manasseh found concrete and practicable formulation in this new edition of the law. The ideas had not disappeared completely. They had been pondered and formulated and set down in writing by certain idealists who looked towards the future and who would not allow themselves to be discouraged by the political and religious chaos prevalent in the reign of Manasseh. This written revision of the law had found its way into the Temple—how or when or why we do not know exactly. It was discovered by Hilkiah when the Temple was undergoing repairs (2 Kgs 22:3–10).

When the book of the law was taken to the king and read in his presence, it caused great bewilderment and consternation: "'Great is the wrath of the Lord . . . that has been kindled against us, because our forefathers did not obey the commands in this book and do all that is laid upon us" (2 Kgs 22:13). It seemed that the clouds had lifted and people could now get a clear look at the horizon. The book pointed out the road that everyone wanted to travel but that no one had been able to locate. It told them *how* to act, giving precise formulation to their vague desires. It set forth a concrete stategy by which they might be guided in their actions.

Everyone soon realized the dimensions of the crisis that they faced (2 Kgs 22:14–17). The whole population was convened, the law was read to them, and they pledged themselves to adhere to it (2 Kgs 23:1–3). The reform movement now had its own charter, and the work could begin in earnest. The whole nation pledged that it would implement each and every one of God's demands in the life of the Hebrew people.

In actual fact it was apparent to everyone that

drastic reform in the life of the nation was crucial and urgent. Religious practice was riddled with superstition. Pagan elements had infiltrated the cult of Yahweh, and there were many shrines in the countryside where Hebrew cultic worship was indistinguishable from the magical cults of the Canaanites. The prophets had unflinchingly denounced the situation, but to little avail. No sooner had Hezekiah died, for example, than Manasseh reintroduced the whole panoply of pagan worship (2 Kgs 21:3–7). The anxious searching and the void in the life of the people was evident in the fact that many of them resorted to such magical elements. The underlying danger was that slowly but surely their notion of God would be perverted. This would inevitably pervert the life of the nation and its reason for being. That is what had happened to Samaria and the Northern Kingdom in 722 B.C. The people had not forgotten, and they were afraid that the same would happen all over again in Judah. The people of the Northern Kingdom had gone to their destruction because they no longer knew who they were or why they were living. Judah desired a preventive medicine. And now they had a document that spelled out how they might live the law of God.

Content of the Reform Charter

Here in brief are the main lines of the reform charter, the new edition of the law, which is now contained in the book of Deuteronomy.

The text presents a discourse by Moses to the Hebrew people shortly before they took possession of the promised land. Actually, the discourse is not addressed to the people living in the time of Moses around 1200 B.C. It is addressed to the people of Jerusalem and Judah around the seventh century B.C. It is addressed to all those who were easy prey to the magical practices and superstitious beliefs that held sway during the reign of Manasseh. Moses speaks to the people in a very direct and personal tone, trying to touch their consciousness and arouse their sense of responsibility. His discourse is meant to help them rediscover their identity as the people of God, their inescapable commitment to God, and the obligations that flow from that commitment. The discourse certainly succeeded with the king, as is evident from his reaction to the reading of it (2 Kgs 22:13).

The line of reasoning in the book of Deuteronomy goes something like this: For the Hebrew people there can be only one God, Yahweh. Yahweh is their one and only Lord and God (Dt 6:4–25). All other deities are useless and worthless, and so they must be rooted out of the country (Dt 6:14–15; 7:25–26). The nation's covenant with Yahweh is not based on what the Hebrew people did for Yahweh but rather on what Yahweh has done for them (Dt 6:20–7:6). It is an obligation of gratitude and love (Dt 7:7–11). Since they have been chosen by Yahweh, all the Hebrews must necessarily observe his commands if they are to benefit from the promises he made to them. This set of basic ideas is the central preoccupation of the first part of the book of Deuteronomy (Dt 1–11). It is followed by a practical application of those ideas to the life of the nation.

Faith in the one God will find expression in one, and only one, sanctuary. All the other places of worship are to be destroyed (Dt 12:2–3). Yahweh, the God of the Hebrew people, can be worshipped only in the place that he himself has chosen (Dt 12:5), and that of course is Jerusalem. It is there that the Hebrews should make their offerings and holocausts (Dt 12:6–7). The proper elements of worship are spelled out in minute detail. Everything is centralized and nothing is left to chance or individual initiative: "You shall not act as we act here today, each of us doing what he pleases" (Dt 22:8). The major concern underlying this approach is to exclude any practice of magic from the liturgy (Dt 12–18).

One of the most important norms was that all Hebrews were to make three pilgrimages to Jerusalem each year to celebrate the three major feasts of the nation (Dt 16:16). This would be an effective way of stimulating the people's awareness of national unity and of giving them instruction about God and the demands of the law.

One must read the book of Deuteronomy itself to get an idea of the vibrant appeal it could make, both then and now, to the consciousness of the people.

Its tone is direct, its style highly suggestive. Yet the reader can also perceive the rigid nature of that liturgical reform, which left nothing to chance.

Clerical Security: Obstacle to Reform

Bound up with the problem of cultic reform was another issue: the livelihood and work of the clergy in the sanctuaries outside Jerusalem. All those sanctuaries, whether dedicated to Yahweh or other deities, had their own priests. For them the sanctuaries represented their only means of making a living. When the Jerusalem clergy decided to eliminate those sanctuaries, they were condemning the rural clergy to hunger and poverty. It seemed to be a vicious circle and an insoluble problem. Hezekiah had attempted to reform the clergy in an earlier day, but to no avail (2 Chr 31:2). Everything took a backward step again during the reign of Manasseh. Without a reasonable solution for the problem of the clergy and their livelihood, other reform solutions would prove fruitless. And no one wants to die of hunger, however alluring and high-minded the reasons for it might be.

The authors of the book of Deuteronomy confronted the problem and offered their own solution, which Josiah tried to implement. A portion of the rural clergy were transferred to Jerusalem, where they were given second-class employment in the Temple (2 Kgs 23:8; Dt 18:6–8). Others were prohibited from establishing themselves in Jerusalem (2 Kgs 23:9) and commended to the charity of the people (Dt 14:27–29). Thus we get a clear glimpse of the rivalry between the clergy in Jerusalem and those outside the city, and we sense the struggle going on between them to win influence over the people. The clergy in the capital city wanted to be the major influence in the country and to centralize cultic worship in their own hands. They could offer sound reasons for this course of action because there was real danger of worship degenerating into magical practice. And if all the clergy were transferred to Jerusalem, then the original group of clergy in the capital would be reduced to a minority faction.

But now the clergy outside Jerusalem found themselves deprived of their normal means of support. Commended to the charity of the people or confined to second-class employment in the Jerusalem Temple, they did not look with favor on the centralizing initiatives of their confreres in Jerusalem. They hardly appreciated being grouped with "the aliens, orphans, and widows" (Dt 14:29). Social security for the clergy was a problem way back then, critical to the success or failure of the reform that was to be implemented.

It becomes apparent, then, that all the legislation enacted during that period of reform reflected the viewpoint of the central administrators in Jerusalem. They had been thinking through the

situation for a long time and had their own clear
awareness. But their outlook did not embody the
feelings and sentiments of the common people and
clergy at the grassroots level. It did not embody
their outlook on the overall problem, and therein
lay the seeds of failure that eventually undermined
the attempted reform.

The Tragic Outcome of the Reform

King Josiah took on the work of reform as a personal mission, doing everything he could to implement it. He travelled through the whole countryside from north to south (2 Kgs 23:4–14), even
penetrating the territory of the defunct Northern
Kingdom (2 Kgs 23:15–20). He was determined to
dismantle all the sanctuaries outside Jerusalem,
whether they were dedicated to Yahweh or to other
gods, so that the Hebrew religion would be healed
from the cancer of superstition and magic. He used
violence, killing priests of the false gods and burning their bones on the destroyed altars (2 Kgs 23:20).
He did much to reform the clergy (2 Kgs 23:8–9),
and he was highly praised: "He did what was right
in the eyes of the Lord; he followed closely in the
footsteps of his forefather David, swerving neither
right nor left" (2 Kgs 22:2).

It is difficult to form a final evaluation of the
reform movement implemented by Josiah because
his unexpected early death prevented him from

carrying out all that he had planned. Incompetent men came after him, and the reforms were never put through completely. Josiah tore down the old structure but he did not have enough time to complete a new one. Once again it was the international situation that influenced the course of internal affairs and gave them an unexpected turn.

Nabopolassar, the ruler of Babylonia, inherited the spirit of combat and independence from his predecessors. He renewed the struggle against the age-old power of the Assyrians. Through a series of lightening-swift attacks he managed to destroy that power in a relatively short time, overthrowing an empire that had been built up over centuries. Assyria came to the end of the line. In 612 B.C., ten years after the revised book of the law had been discovered in the Temple at Jerusalem and the work of reform had been initiated by Josiah, the Assyrian capital of Nineveh was taken by the Babylonians and totally destroyed. The event was something like the dropping of the first atomic bomb; it marked the end of a whole era and the start of a new one. The Assyrians and their surviving forces retreated northward into present-day Syria and made a last-ditch attempt to ward off the inevitable.

As is often the case in international politics, this changed situation brought about realignments in the balance of power. Egypt, the old enemy of Assyria, now sided with Assyria to maintain a favorable balance of power in the areas. The pharaoh

Necho sent an Egyptian army to reinforce the rem-
nants of the Assyrian force now entrenched in
Syria, and this Egyptian army had to pass through
the territory of King Josiah. Feeling a bit too cocky,
perhaps, Josiah now felt he could make a positive
impact on the international scene. Desiring to hasten the total collapse of Assyria, and to undermine
the power of Egypt, he decided to do battle with
Egyptian forces as they passed through the
strategic city of Megiddo. But Josiah had miscalcu-
lated. His army was routed in their first encounter
with the Egyptians (2 Kgs 23:29), and he himself
was mortally wounded. He was carried back to
Jerusalem, and there he died. The people buried
him amid great lamentation, for they saw him as a
true friend and hero of the Hebrew nation (2 Chr
35:23–24). It is said that the prophet Jeremiah himself delivered the funeral elegy over the bier of the
young king, whose death killed the last vestiges of
hope in the Hebrew people (2 Chr 35:25). Josiah was
only thirty-nine years old when he died (2 Kgs
22:1).

Twelve years of intense reform work came to a
standstill with the unexpected death of Josiah. The
year was 609 B.C. On his way back from the military
campaign in Syria, the pharaoh came through
Jerusalem and took control of the government of
Judah. He placed his own hand-picked candidate
on the throne (2 Chr 36:1–4), and the decline began.
Twenty-two years later, in 587 B.C., the city of

Jerusalem was taken by Nebuchadnezzar, the king of Babylon, who subjected it to total destruction. The independence of the people was destroyed, not to be revived until A.D. 1947 with the creation of the state of Israel. Today the Israelis find themselves fighting similar battles within a similar web of political interplay among the great powers.

Evaluation of the Reform Movement

The reform movement died with the young king who had sponsored it. What was the fatal flaw which doomed it to failure? Was it international politics, the incompetence of Josiah's successors, Josiah himself, or the "reform charter"? If the reform had been put through precisely to avoid the disaster that eventually befell Judah, why was it unable to achieve its goals? Was the movement too weak or too forceful? Was it hopeless from the start?

There is one curious fact surrounding the reform movement. The prophet Jeremiah, the great religious figure of the day, was present from the very beginning of the movement. He urged conversion of the Hebrew people, and he lamented the death of the young king. Yet in his prophetical pronouncements we do not find him giving wholehearted support to everything that was being done in the name of reform. He did not identify himself with the reform movement that was carried to its logical conclusion by King Josiah. Why?

In those days changes generally took place much more slowly than they do today, yet catastrophe befell Judah in a matter of twenty years after Josiah's death. Did the reform movement hasten the catastrophe or slow it up? It is difficult to form a fully rounded judgment on the question because sufficient data is lacking. The fact does demand some explanation, however, as it is of some relevance to us today: At present the Catholic Church is involved in a great effort at reform with a whole host of factors and events involved, both inside and outside the Church, both on the national and international level.

With regard to a work of art, we can make all sorts of studies in an attempt to understand fully the message the artist intended to convey. That does not mean that the message deduced by the art critic is the same as the one intended by the artist. But at least the effort of the critic is within the perspective of the artist, since the artist is trying to stimulate the reflection of the viewer and confront him with his own consciousness and awareness. So it is with any attempt to explain the Bible and the facts related in it. The comments of the exegetes are not important, for their presentation is relative. The important thing is that the exegetes, in their capacity as interpreters, be able to let loose the light and power of God's word so that it can operate on the conscience and awareness of other people. Indeed others may arrive at their own conclusions, quite different from those offered by the exegete. That does not matter much. What is important is that people stop and reflect, comparing their lives and deeds with the word of God, that they examine their actions in the light of God's word.

The Fatal Miscalculation

The book of Deuteronomy does indeed present a new approach to living the faith, and it did arise as a response to real needs. Unfortunately, however, it embodied the response of a minority group who chose to impose their solution on everyone in a rather precipitous way. Their solution did not embody the thinking of the whole people, even though most people did want reform. The reform movement plowed ahead at full speed when the light flashed yellow; it should have proceeded with caution. Hence it hastened the catastrophe it was trying to prevent.

When we are trying to get people to change their outlook and their religious practices, we should not rush ahead too rapidly. A bit of patient waiting is advisable if we want to avoid disaster. The Deuteronomic reform was a drastic one, and it closely followed the ground plan laid out by the theologians in Jerusalem. While it certainly left a deep mark on the life of the Hebrew people, it never got beyond the level of theory. In practice it did not work, at least not at that particular time. Only after the exile in Babylon did it become a matter of real praxis.

The Deuteronomic reform remained a reform imposed on the people from above, based on a prefabricated scheme. The common people with their own aspirations did not really have a say in this reform movement which was undertaken with such intensity. Hence they never really accepted it as their own. The reform died with the king who had been promoting it, and it failed to impress itself on the hearts of the people. The common people were not so readily given to facile reasoning and purely intellectual arguments, however simple and clear-cut those arguments might seem to be. The problem of faith confronting the people at the time was framed in very practical terms through Josiah's reform project; and when theory is applied in a drastic fashion to that sort of situation, it may well fail to provide a sound solution. Theory can have great value over the long run as a potent force for consciousness-raising. But when the real-life situation is not taken into serious consideration, then the direct implementation of drastic theoretical solutions will not work. They are not fully comprehended and accepted by the people, and so they fail.

The fact is that King Josiah did not seem to show much consideration for, or understanding of, the concrete situation of the people and the clergy living outside Jerusalem. He followed the norms of a prefabricated plan without asking himself whether they were really being implemented in a viable way. The success of the reform movement depended on the collaboration of the Hebrew people as a group, but they were not seriously consulted in the process of trying to work out a solution to the problem. It was they who would have to support the clergy, give tithes to the Temple, make the three pilgrimages to Jerusalem each year, and observe all the other prescriptions.

All the public forms of divine worship were centralized in Jerusalem; other forms were prohibited or strictly controlled. Everything was planned down to the most minute details. Although well intentioned, the sudden and brusquely implemented reform deprived the common people of the only prop they could count on in those tumultuous times. However spurious it might have been, their traditional form of worship had helped them to come face to face with themselves and with God. But once the Deuteronomic reform had been effected, they would find themselves outside the law if they continued their traditional religious practices. Now deprived of the way of adoring God that had been theirs for generations, and not appreciating the reasoning behind the new forms of worship, the common people could no longer feel at home with themselves or with God. In practice it was impossible for them to get to Jerusalem each year, and in any case the three pilgrimages were not enough to satisfy their intense religious yearnings. At a much later date the establishment of the local synagogue overcame this serious flaw and made it possible for the Hebrew people successfully to implement the reforms spelled out in Deuteronomy.

The end result in the time of Josiah, however, was not a happy one. The Hebrew people found themselves on the sidelines of the nation's official worship. A great void had been created, with nothing to fill it but an abstract idea. The offical law of the land reduced the people to a life without God and personal orientation in the midst of religious and political chaos. Thus the reform had a great impact on the people in many respects, but the rigorous application of the new norms lacked grass-roots support among the people and hence could not produce solid results. The common people were trodden underfoot and their religious practice was squelched. So the premature death of Josiah opened up the floodgates, and the outlawed pagan practices returned with redoubled force to fill the vacuum created by the reform movement.

It is noteworthy that Jeremiah did not rubber-stamp the reform movement. As far as we can tell, he was a man of the people and the great religious leader of his day, but he did not fully and explicitly endorse all the elements of the reform. If ever there was a man who was courageous in criticizing religious abuses, it was Jeremiah. But in a period marked by great confusion, it is not always easy to take a well-defined stand as to what ought to be done. It may be easy enough to say what ought *not* be done, but it may be unwise to spell out precisely what must be done and officially prohibit any other course of action.

It is not a matter of being faithful *solely* to God. Fidelity to God demands that one be faithful to the people as well. In other words, God's primary concern is the well-being and happiness of human beings. God wants them to grow and attain self-fulfillment. At times people may choose to equate fidelity with a legalistic concern for norms and rules. Such concern, allegedly to purify faith, may be good and proper; but it is not always what God really desires. A father's main concern is not that his son have precise and correct ideas about who his father is but rather that his son be happy and prosperous in life. Insofar as he is happy, thanks to the goodness of his father, he will acquire sound ideas about his father.

Reverence for God is not detached from our happiness and well-being. It is not enough to ask *what* God wants us to do. We must also ask *how* God wants us to carry out the tasks he asks of us. The greater errors are usually committed in connection with the second requirement rather than the first. We stay loyal to the abstract doctrine, but we do not adhere to God's outlook in the way we live the doctrine and put it into practice. The law contained in the book of Deuteronomy did and still does contain sound doctrine, for the Bible retains it and we Christians still ponder it today. But the way in which the Deuteronomic reformers implemented it in the time of Josiah precluded any chance of real success. They did not implement it in the right way. They acted in wholehearted obedience and with the best of intentions, but that is not always enough.

Conclusion

In conveying this complicated history of a reform movement, the Bible clearly provides us with sound guidelines for orientation and critical thinking. It shows us that the word of God is deeply interwoven with human history and dependent on free human decisions, so much so that it may fail to achieve its objective because of them. Thus the Bible presents us with the great mystery of human history, without explaining it to us. In the Bible we find an unshakeable faith that history, given direction and impetus by the word of God, is a victorious history. This certainty led the people of the Bible to make decisions and act upon them. At the same time, however, the human decisions and actions sometimes obscured the presence of God's word and nullified its impact. What happened in the time of Josiah was a prelude to what would happen when the Word-made-flesh arrived. He was eliminated from the human scene, slain on a cross. In his seeming defeat he displayed his invincible power.

All of this merely serves to heighten a sense of responsibility in those who truly believe in God.

The Deuteronomic reform started off well and ended up badly because it failed to respect the people. Its complex history indicates that the people of the Bible had a history just like any other nation did. They lived amid an atmosphere of confusion, with fears and hopes of their own. The prophets appeared, scanning the horizon and gropingly trying to detect the signs sent by God. They did not always see their way clearly. But in their company the Hebrew people lived through their ups and downs and reached the goal that God had chosen for them. The people of the Bible did not have a direct telephone connection with God, but they were convinced that God was present amid everything that was happening to them. Their tortured history is an impressive quest for God.

7

Jeremiah: Evasion
Never Solves Anything

Even though Jeremiah lived in historical circumstances very different from ours, there is something
that makes us feel one with him. He alerts us to
certain aspects of life in which we do not usually
tend to sense or see the summons of God. When we
take a close look at Jeremiah, he does not seem to be
a figure of the past at all. It is almost as if we might
run into him on a street corner.

Jeremiah's Situation

Let us first take a brief look at the historical and
social situation of Jeremiah's day. We have already
considered it in some detail in the previous chapter
when we dealt with the reform movement. Here we
are concerned mainly with the period that extends
from the death of King Josiah (609 B.C.) to the exile
of the people of Judah into Babylon (587 B.C.).

On the *international scene*, world politics under-
went a real change. Assyria and Egypt, which had
been the two predominant world powers, lost their
imperial control of the area. A third world power,
awesome and threatening, had come to dominate.
In the year 612 B.C., the Babylonians destroyed
Nineveh, the capital of Assyria. It was an event that
sent shock waves through the Near East, shock
waves of delight in many instances (see the book of
Nahum). The people of Judah viewed the changed
situation with great pleasure, and they had even
attempted to help it along so that they in turn might
benefit from the result. As we noted previously,
King Josiah led out his army in 609 B.C. to prevent
the pharaoh of Egypt from going to the aid of the
retreating Assyrian army. His army was defeated
and he himself was fatally wounded, but the com-
bined forces of Assyria and Egypt were eventually
decimated. From 609 B.C. on, the road lay open for
the advance of Babylon.

The changed international situation had
repercussions on the politics of Judah. One faction in
Judah favored Babylon, another favored Egypt.
Three months after the death of Josiah, who was
pro-Babylonian, the Egyptian pharaoh dethroned
his pro-Babylonian successor (Jehoahaz) and
placed a pro-Egyptian king (Jehoiakim) on the
throne of Judah. With the crowning of Jehoiakim
(609–598), Babylon became a serious threat to
Judah. Once the Babylonian forces had won victory
over Pharaoh Necho, Judah became a vassal state

of Babylon (in 605 B.C.). Pro-Egyptian intrigue in Judah led to a revolt against Babylon which was gradually crushed. From the time of this revolt against Babylon (602 B.C.) to the destruction of Jerusalem (587 B.C.), confusion reigned in Judah. There developed an almost pathological fear of Babylon, the "disaster from the north" (Jer 1:14–15). The country was marked by intrigue, political maneuvering, and sabotage. No one seemed able to think straight, and ridiculous solutions were proposed to counter the danger that threatened the country.

The *national situation* was also grave. The sudden early death of King Josiah, the nation's beloved leader, was a heavy blow. It killed the last vestiges of hope in the hearts of many people. The reform movement sparked by his leadership (see chapter 4 and chapter 6) did not move forward. Decay set in, and incompetent kings assumed the throne. Amid this atmosphere of general uncertainty, everybody looked out for himself and injustice became a growing cancer.

The nation sought to obtain some measure of security by entering military alliances with Egypt and pretending that there was no danger from Babylon. Some insisted that all was well when in fact nothing was well (Jer 6:14). The nation's happy façade was an attempt to conceal real feelings of terror (Jer 8:11). This false political front was shrouded in the protective mantle of official religion. People felt they would be safe if they were faithful in carrying out the rites and feasts of the liturgical year (Jer 7:10). And it was easy enough to find priests and prophets who would sanction that approach and assure the leaders that their solution was the correct one (Jer 8:10). Religion in Judah truly became the opiate of the people, who believed what the false prophets were telling them: "Prosperity shall be yours. . . . No disaster shall befall you" (Jer 23:17). But empty rites, lifeless ceremonies, and worthless promises do not provide defense against the enemy. The ultimate disaster moved closer and closer while religion was used to defend selfish group interests.

A Prophetic Vocation

In the small village of Anathoth, about six kilometers north of Jerusalem, there lived a youth named Jeremiah. He came from a priestly family (Jer 1:1) and was probably a descendant of Abiathar, a high priest under David who was later driven out of his post by Solomon (1 Kgs 2:26–27). The tradition of the Hebrew people coursed through Jeremiah's veins. He felt the tragic situation of the nation with great personal intensity and recognized the absurdity of the official solutions. They did not go to the roots of the problem.

Insofar as we can judge from Jeremiah's later writings, his faith in God led him to view the situation with a critical eye. He knew what his faith demanded, and he knew that the makeshift solutions of the time would not be effective. His vision was very simple, even simplistic, but it was wide-ranging. The existing situation was clear proof that the Hebrew people had abandoned the pathway of God. Injustice was securely entrenched in power, and it had even reached the king's throne (Jer 22:13–19). This caused Jeremiah to doubt if there was even one person in Jerusalem who was still practicing justice (Jer 5:1). As one oracle puts it: "They run from one sin to another, and for me they care nothing. This is the very word of the Lord" (Jer 9:3).

The simple explanation was that the people had abandoned God (Jer 2:13). Instead of serving the God of the nation, who wanted the people to practice justice (Jer 7:5–6), all were following their own version of God. There were as many gods as there were towns in Judah, as many altars as there were streets in Jerusalem itself (Jer 11:13). And so the nation headed toward total disintegration.

In such a situation the politics of the ostrich would not help at all. It would do no good to evade responsibility, to seek protection and security in empty-headed religiosity or dubious military alliances. The evil had to be attacked at its roots: "Administer justice betimes, rescue the victim from his oppressor, lest the fire of my fury blaze up and burn unquenched because of your evil doings" (Jer

21:12). All the proposed solutions were equally futile. Instead of warding off "the disaster from the north," they only brought it closer. The people and their leaders were digging their own grave. They did not seem to realize the false solutions would only hasten disaster.

This critical vision of reality aroused Jeremiah to a sense of his own personal responsibility. Something had to be done. God would want that. The problem obsessed Jeremiah until one day in the kitchen he saw a cauldron tipping towards the south: "The Lord came to me a second time: 'What is it that you see?' 'A cauldron,' I said, 'on a fire fanned by the wind; it is tilted away from the north' " (Jer 1:13). Facts and events began to speak a message when they were connected with the problem which so concerned him: "From the north disaster shall flare up against all who live in this land" (Jer 1:14).

That is how Jeremiah's vocation arose. He came to see clearly that God was summoning him to speak out the truth to his people, that this was the mission that had been entrusted to him from his mother's womb (Jer 1:5). He is frightened: "Ah! Lord God, . . . I do not know how to speak; I am only a child" (Jer 1:6). But he had to put fear aside because the might of God would be with him: "Fear none of them, for I am with you and will keep you safe" (Jer 1:8). Jeremiah was to be "a fortified city, a pillar of iron, a wall of bronze to stand fast against the whole land" (Jer 1:18). No one will get the better of him because he was on the side of right and truth: "They will make war on you but shall not overcome you, for I am with you and will keep you safe" (Jer 1:19).

So Jeremiah set out on his mission, the mission that had slowly matured in his mind as a personal conviction. He was sure that it came from God, the Lord of his people.

Jeremiah in Action

In an atmosphere of pervasive anxiety Jeremiah remained calm. He forthrightly denounced the falseness of official policy and politics and paid no heed to the pronouncements of opportunists and false prophets (Jer 28:1–17; 23:9–40). He offered no guarantees of protection whatsoever. There was no guarantee in the Temple, for he believed it was a tragic mistake to seek reassurance in the existence of the Temple. God no longer dwelt there, but had become a wandering alien in his own land (Jer 14:8). The Temple would be destroyed as if it were just another building (Jer 7:12–14). God no longer wanted to be on familiar terms with the Israelites (Jer 7:15). Circumcision (Jer 9:24), sacrifices (Jer 14:12), fasting (Jer 14:12), and prayer (Jer 11:14): none of these practices on which the people relied for security were of any real use. Not even the great figures of the past, such as Moses and Samuel,

could persuade God to have pity on the Hebrew
people (Jer 15:1). The law was no longer a source of
protection because lying had turned God's law into
an instrument of deceit and oppression (Jer 8:8–9).
The king, once the apple of God's eye, had become
ineffective: "Coniah, son of Jehoiakim, king of
Judah, shall be the signet-ring on my right hand no
longer. Yes, Coniah, I will pull you off" (Jer 22:24).
The king will have no line of successors (Jer 22:30).

The logical conclusion was that God had ceased
to dwell in Jerusalem (Jer 8:19). There was no sense
in saying that all was well because things were
getting worse and worse (Jer 8:11). There was no
sense thinking that Egypt might be interested in
offering aid (Jer 37:7). "Egypt will fail you as Assyria
did; you shall go out from here, each of you with his
hands above his head" (Jer 2:36–37). All the proposed solutions were mere evasions, and evasion is
never a solution. It hastens the approaching danger
instead of warding it off.

At this point one might well challenge Jeremiah
himself: "Okay, critic, what solution do you yourself propose?" Jeremiah had no solution to offer.
Decay had set in, and the present setup would be
swept away: "Can the Nubian change his skin, or
the leopard its spots? And you? Can you do good,
you who are schooled in evil?" (Jer 13:23). Sin was
all-pervasive (Jer 17:1–2). The people could not
change their way of life even if they wanted to (Jer
18:11–12). The fact was that fidelity had disap-

peared (Jer 7:27–28). So God will "shatter this people and this city as one shatters an earthen vessel so that it cannot be mended" (Jer 19:11). Where, then, are the people to go? The Lord's answer is appalling: "Those who are for death shall go to their death, and those for the sword to the sword; those who are for famine to famine, and those for captivity to captivity" (Jer 15:2). The only escape from this fate would be to surrender to the approaching enemy (Jer 27:12; 38:17–18). This was the advice that Jeremiah had to offer to anyone willing to listen to him!

Jeremiah's other counsels about doing good and practicing justice seemed to fall into the void. A man who spoke such alarmist ideas was dangerous and subversive. His words upset the people, demoralized the city dwellers, and sapped the courage of the soldiers who were to defend the city against the advancing Babylonians (Jer 38:4). This man had to be put out of the way because he only spoke words of terror (Jer 20:10). Some plotted his capture. One relatively quiet evening, after a protracted Babylonian siege of Jerusalem, Jeremiah was taken as he was heading out of the city (Jer 37:11–16). He was accused of going over to the other side, but he vigorously denied the charge (Jer 37:14). His explanations were to no avail. He was hurled into prison, and he greatly feared that he would be killed (Jer 37:20).

But the imprisonment of Jeremiah did not solve

anything. Whether on the loose or in prison, his kind of person gets under people's skin. Actually, the situation grew worse, because Jeremiah's imprisonment caused further division between the leaders of the nation (Jer 37–38). Both his friends and his enemies were afraid of him, as we can see from the secret meeting between the king and him. The king begged him not to tell anyone about it (Jer 38:24–26).

Jeremiah was a person who did not see "faith in God" as alienated from life. To have faith in God was to live a solid and fruitful human life. He saw the summons of God in happenings around him, in both national and international events. And since all his countrymen claimed to believe in God, Jeremiah committed himself to the task of showing them what that faith entailed. His message was painful because the people did not want to admit the truth of it. His forthright words and clear-cut actions cut them to the quick. Some wanted to silence him at all costs.

Consequences of Commitment

Looking at the figure of Jeremiah from the safe distance of time, we admire him. Those who saw him close up were bewildered by his violent suffering and unfailing fidelity to his mission. He had not asked for that mission; it had gradually grown inside him as a response to God's summons (Jer

20:7–9). One must suffer a great deal to say what Jeremiah said: "A curse on the day when I was born! Be it forever unblessed, the day when my mother bore me, . . . because death did not claim me before birth, and my mother did not become my grave, her womb great with me for ever" (Jer 20:14, 17).

He was the victim of plots and attacks (Jer 18:18), "a man doomed to strike, with the whole world against me" (Jer 15:10). He labored and struggled for twenty-three years without the least success (Jer 25:3). He complains bitterly: "I have forsaken the house of Israel, I have cast off my own people. I have given my beloved into the power of her foes. My own people have turned on me like a lion from the scrub, roaring against me" (Jer 12:7–8). Jeremiah suffers in lonely isolation. Everyone has turned against him. His own relatives betray him (Jer 12:6), and his fellow citizens of Anathoth want to kill him (Jer 11:18–21). The nation's priests, the other prophets, and many of the people want to put him to death (Jer 26:8). Eventually he is hurled into a fetid pit, from which one of his friends rescues him (Jer 38:1–13). His suffering seems useless and absurd because he has no results to show for it after twenty-three years of work.

But in the midst of all this suffering Jeremiah is sustained by a force which no human being can crush. It makes him a fortified city, a pillar of iron, and a wall of bronze. For Jeremiah is sure of one thing: "The Lord is on my side, strong and ruthless" (Jer 20:11). His lot was harsh and he often fought against it, but at bottom he chose it and took delight in it. He knew it was the proper road for him. When his mission brought him suffering, he recalled the moment when his vocation came to him: "O Lord, thou hast duped me, and I have been thy dupe; thou hast outwitted me and hast prevailed" (Jer 20:7).

Without honor in his own lifetime, this man would eventually become an image of the Messiah to come: a man of sorrows who would shoulder the sinful guilt of us all (Mt 8:17; Is 53:3–4). It often happens that a person who seemed to extinguish people's hopes while alive becomes a symbol of universal hope after his death.

Jeremiah's Contribution to God's Plan

Jeremiah had no human being to confide in during his lifetime, so he confided in God. He thus contributed to the interiorization of religion, to its becoming a religion "of the heart": that is, a very personal force at work in the inner depths of a person and not just relating to external, superficial acts.

Jeremiah did this not so much by his teachings as by his way of living. He had to suffer in order to overcome the obstacles facing his mission, in order to succeed in life. He managed to lead a successful life because in and through his suffering he learned to apply all the collective values of the nation's faith to his own personal life. Suffering led him to interiorize religion and enabled him to grow as a human being.

In his prayer—and there is a great deal of prayer in his writings—Jeremiah did not put on an act. He said what was in his mind and heart, even when it sounded like vengeance and despair. He even came to curse the day that he was born. He grew in the life of faith by living out his personal drama and enduring a life of solitude. (Faithful to his unique vocation, he never married.) All the values of past tradition were assimilated by Jeremiah in his own way.

This becomes clear to anyone who reads the sections known as the "Confessions of Jeremiah" (Jer 11:18–12:6; 15:10–21; 17:14–18; 18:18–23; 20:7–18; 12:7–13). Through his suffering there emerged his own personal and individual conscience over against the collective conscience of the nation. He found himself because he came into contact with the absolute "I" of God. In Jeremiah the Hebrew religion became more adult. He marked the beginning of the reform movement that would be carried forward by Hasidim, the lowly people of God to which Mary and Elizabeth would later belong.

Clearly reflected in the life and writing of Jeremiah is religion made flesh. Jeremiah was courageous enough to point out God's appeals in real life. For him religion was not an abstract system. It was human beings journeying steadfastly toward the future under the initiative of faith. Jeremiah was even bold enough to point out God's summons in international events. He clearly embodied faith in the fact that God holds the world and its destiny in his hands.

In Jeremiah we also find the conviction that the world will be what human beings make of it with their freedom. One cannot appeal to God to justify a situation of decay that is contrary to human well-being.

During his lifetime Jeremiah was a center of controversy. After his death he became a symbol of hope. When a later author, during the period of exile in Babylon, describes the future Messiah, he probably has the figure of Jeremiah in mind (Is 53).

8

Wisdom Literature: The Yearning for Life and the Fact of Death

In this chapter we tackle a new section of the Old Testament. We considered certain aspects of the *historical* books in the first four chapters. In chapters 5 and 7 we spoke about the *prophetical* books. Now we shall consider the *sapiential* books.

The title of this chapter focuses on *one* major theme that runs through the sapiential books. (Another major preoccupation of the sapiential writers is the existence of suffering and evil in the world, but we shall discuss that theme in the next chapter in connection with the book of Job).

Let us begin our discussion with a brief consideration of how the sapiential books came into being.

Origin of the Sapiential Books

One group of books in the Old Testament is known as the *sapiential* books. They include: Proverbs, Ecclesiasticus (or Sirach), Ecclesiastes, the Song of Songs, Job, and Wisdom. Some include the book of Psalms in this grouping, but we shall consider the Psalms separately in chapter 10.

There is a big difference between the historical and prophetical books and the sapiential books. The former embody the new thinking that various religious leaders communicated to the people for the improvement of their lives. The latter embody the long-standing thinking of the common people, now expressed in organized fashion so that it might improve the lives of those who read it. Thus we have two different styles of thinking. The former confronts us with reasoned thinking which moves from the outside to the inside, from above to below. In the latter case we are confronted with reasoned thinking which moves from the inside to the outside, from below to above.

We find these two different styles of thinking operative today. Akin to the prophetical writings is the doctrine of the Church formulated and embodied in catechetical, conciliar, and papal documents. People read those documents to find guidance in life. Akin to the process evident in the sapiential books is people's quest for a way to improve their lives. In this case people start from the data of life experiences, which have been illuminated by the social disciplines. They study such subjects as anthropology, psychology, sociology, and economics as they relate to life.

Even today it is often the sapiential books that are most favored by average lay people and least studied by the clergy. Perhaps some unconscious class prejudice is responsible for the fact that the educated clergy—and that would include theologians and biblical exegetes—often prefer the historical and prophetical books of the Bible to the sapiential books. This predilection certainly does not help them to gain a solid, well-rounded acquaintance with the whole corpus of divine revelation, for some of that corpus has found expression in the thinking of the common people which is contained in the sapiential books.

The wisdom thinking contained in the sapiential books is part of a broad cultural phenomenon that typifies the whole ancient Middle East. In addition to the ancient Hebrews, the people of Egypt, Assyria, and Babylonia also had their own sapiential literature. Wisdom thinking does not mean, first and foremost, some sort of abstract intellectual virtue or knowledge. It refers to a basic aptitude for living life well and acting in a sensible way. It is a "philosophy of life." It represents a certain attitude toward life that was typical of those ancient peoples. In itself it had little to do with religion, just as modern thinking about such subjects as anthropology and economics has little to do with the religious convictions of those who work in those subjects. The fact that people are religious believers does not make them better mathematicians or economists.

Religious conviction does not play a major role in their thinking as mathematicians or economists, even though it may ultimately affect the way they live their lives as professional persons. It is in the latter sense that faith does in fact have a role to play in our world, even as it did in the world of biblical times. That also explains why wisdom thinking took a different turn in the Bible than it did in other sapiential literature.

The Israelites were in the same basic situation as their neighbors. They pondered life with the same basic principles in mind, and they did not hesitate to borrow passages from the wisdom thinking of other nations. The Hebrews borrowed from the Egyptians (Prv 22:17–23:11), even as sociologists in the Third World today often borrow ideas from sociologists in developed nations.

At the core of wisdom thinking we find the people, who kept reflecting on life and looking for answers to basic questions. How are we to live? What should we do to succeed in life? How should we behave? These are the questions of serious, thoughtful people who want to know how to act meaningfully in life so that they will not be overwhelmed by it. The search for wisdom is a search for the norms and values that rule human existence. People want to find out what these norms and values are so that they can integrate them into their lives and thus make progress in their existential situation.

The search began humbly enough among the common people. Its beginnings can be found in proverbs, which are still passed around today. It took on more complex and scientific form in such writings as the book of Job and the book of Wisdom.

The chief concern of wisdom thinking is to confront the evils that beset life, to form the growing younger generation, and thus *give direction* to human life. The only solutions accepted were those that had proved to be viable in the concrete praxis of life. A typical example of this basic outlook can be found in the book of Ecclesiastes, which is a veritable textbook on the way that the wise person proceeds in his exploration.

The root source of wisdom thinking, its original milieu, is the realm of family life and family training. Parents tried to help their children open their eyes to reality and look at life objectively. Wisdom thinking was a store of accumulated experiences handed down from parent to child over many generations. The pedagogical approach used was rather interesting. Initially the wise person, the sage, was one who had a special knack for formulating some lesson about life in a pointed saying. This gave rise to popular proverbs, which served as foundation stones for life and embodied the values that had been discovered or worked out by certain individuals in the community. Here are some examples of proverbs from the Bible:

A merry heart makes a cheerful countenance,
but low spirits sap a man's strength. (Prv 17:22)

To answer a question before you have heard it out
is both stupid and insulting. (Prv 18:13)

The poor man speaks in a tone of entreaty,
and the rich man gives a harsh answer. (Prv 18:23)

Wealth makes many friends,
but a man without means loses the friend he has.
(Prv 19:4)

In the life of the downtrodden every day is wretched,
but to have a glad heart is a perpetual feast. (Prv 15:15)

Even a fool, if he holds his peace, is thought wise;
keep your mouth shut and show your good sense.
(Prv 17:28)

The sluggard plunges his hand in the dish
but will not so much as lift it to his mouth. (Prv 19:24)

Like a gold ring in a pig's snout
is a beautiful woman without good sense. (Prv 11:22)

There are many similar proverbs in the Bible. A proverb expresses some elementary experience in life by way of a *mashal* (i.e., a comparison). Such proverbs forced people to think and helped them discover values in life. They are replete with good sense, learned at a father's knee and in circles of friends. They helped give orientation and direction to the children, not as rote formulas but as illuminators of basic values. They were concerned

with the things of immediate interest in life: how to
behave, how to deal with other people. There was
little philosophic speculation in them, but they possessed a profundity that is typical of popular wisdom all over the world. Examples of the topics
treated proverbially in the book of Ecclesiasticus
(Sirach) include patience, almsgiving, false security, the unbridled tongue, friendship, fighting,
liberty, social relationships, respect for woman,
fear of God, table etiquette, value of caution, pru-
dence in the presence of the powerful, the dangers
of wine and loose women, making loans, keeping a
friend's secret, and so forth.

The Institutionalization of Wisdom Thinking

Gradually this wisdom thinking grew in scope
and content, extending to every sector of life. Moving out from the family circle, it became an object of
careful exploration and lost something of its spon-
taneous character. It became institutionalized, taking its place alongside such institutions as the
priesthood and the prophetic office. It would now
help to ensure the proper organization of society.

In the hands of the king, this institutionalized
wisdom thinking became a tool of government, and
it began to be associated with the figure of King
Solomon, the sage par excellence (1 Kgs 4:27–54). It
would now help the king to govern his people even

as it had once helped parents to guide their children.

With this change in status and milieu, wisdom thinking became an object of scholarly meditation and study. Alongside the age-old popular sayings, there arose scholarly tracts on the same basic subjects. The concrete cast of the older proverbs gave way to intellectual probing into the basic philosophy of life that underlay the whole process of wisdom thinking. (We see a similar process at work today with regard to politics, for example. People have practiced politics for countless centuries, but it is only recently that we have seen the rise of schools of political science.)

Thus we can see a gradual evolution in the praxis of wisdom thinking within the Bible itself. The various sapiential books bear witness to different stages in the process. Let us consider each briefly.

Proverbs. This book is a compilation of popular old proverbs. But the final editors or compilers appended a preface to the whole work, in which they tried to explain the nature and origin of wisdom (Prv 1–9). The first nine chapters were written much later, and so they are more profoundly theoretical than the rest of the book. The proverbs themselves come from the family circle and the daily life of the people, and they deal with the upbringing of children and the concrete problems of life.

The Song of Songs. Everything indicates that we

are dealing here with a compilation of popular songs about love. Some sage felt that those songs would help to give concrete expression to God's love for human beings and their love for God. Twelve of the songs were incorporated into this book, which has always been a favorite of commentators.

Ecclesiasticus, or Sirach. This book presents wisdom thinking at the point where it is moving out of the family circle. It contains many small treatises on the most varied matters. The proverbs are now beginning to be organized into various categories. But in this book we see that people have not yet begun to engage in philosophical reflection on the origin and source of wisdom. The concrete aspect predominates.

Ecclesiastes. This book was put together by one of the official government sages. He expresses his deep frustration with the many different attitudes human beings hold towards life. None of them satisfies him. He has carefully examined them all, and he has reached the conclusion that everything is vanity. Here and there he inserts a proverb on God's activity in life, indicating that he has not completely lost his faith in life and its author, God.

Job. Here we have wisdom thinking in its loftiest literary expression. It tackles one of the problems that most preoccupied the sages: the suffering of the just and upright person. The treatment takes the form of a drama, and the old proverbial approach is left behind. The experience of a human being who has suffered greatly finds expression in this book.

Wisdom. It is the latest of the sapiential books, written sometime in the first century B.C. It is also the most profound treatment of the true origin of Wisdom, which it attributes to God. It was written in Egypt, and its style shows marked Greek influence.

The Message of the Sapiential Books

When we read the sapiential books, particularly those written earlier (e.g., Proverbs and Ecclesiasticus), we soon notice that they do not say much about God. They talk about life. We also notice that most of what they say about life could have been discovered by anyone who does a bit of reflecting. They do not seem to contain anything extraordinary. They simply deal with the ordinary affairs of everyday life. So why are these books in the Bible? Why did God take the trouble to inspire such works? We can find similar thoughts, just as profound, in the wisdom literature of Egypt and Babylon. What is the purpose of all this wisdom thinking in the Bible?

The whole atmosphere of wisdom thinking influenced the outlook and thinking habits of people in antiquity much as science influences our mentality today. The seed of God's word was sown in soil that was interlaced with such wisdom thinking. There the tree of divine revelation would take root and grow. It took a long time before the sages perceived the value of divine revelation for their own wisdom thinking. That does not mean they had ceased to be people of faith. It simply means that at first their faith did not exert much influence on their wisdom thinking, on the way they pondered life and sought to find values in it. The same would be true of a professional anthropologist today. Even though he might be a man of deep faith and religious conviction, the basic principles of his professional discipline would not be greatly influenced by that fact.

As time went on, however, wisdom thinking became aware of the limited usefulness of the solutions it proposed for human problems. It gradually became more open to the word of divine revelation that had been handed down by priests and prophets and enshrined in other books of the Bible. The sages began to realize that divine revelation had some value for their own explorations into life. They took over the word of God as a useful tool for discovering true wisdom. Thus, without sacrificing its own methodology and patterns of thought, wisdom thinking was deeply influenced by the priests and prophets in the way it approached its reflection on its own origin and orientation. It came to see God as the ultimate origin and goal of all the wisdom thinking that guided human life.

The God in question was not just any deity. This

was the God of Abraham, of the one who initiated and gave direction to the history of the Hebrew people. This same God was at the source of the laws and values that ruled their lives. Suddenly everything became clear. God's law, the Mosaic law, was identical with wisdom, as Psalm 119 plainly states. Thus the whole area of investigation was greatly expanded. Now it was not just present-day life and its problems that deserved to be analyzed. All of past history also deserved consideration, because therein God had left traces of his wisdom.

So we begin to find considerations of past history in the sapiential books (Sir 44–50; Wis 10–19). In this case, history is not seen from the standpoint of priest or prophet but from the standpoint of the common people insofar as they have been imbued with the features of wisdom thinking. This line of thought finds summary expression in the Prologue to Saint John's Gospel, which tells us that the creative divine Word at the source of all life is also the salvific divine Word that gives direction to all history. Both life and history are rooted in God, and embodied in Jesus Christ, the Word-made-flesh (Jn 1:1–14).

This discovery of God as the origin and end of wisdom placed the age-old proverbs in a new light. They were now considered the first lowly steps on the ladder of life leading up to God. Thus the sapiential books in the Bible bear witness to an optimistic vision of life: For the person who has eyes to see, all reality can serve as a mirror of God. The sapiential books bear perduring witness to the fact that the locus of our encounter with God is the ordinary life of every day, the things that well up from the depths of concrete experience. The great treasure possessed by all of us is the life we are living. The sapiential books urge us to look for God in life itself, not in rites and ceremonies, vigils and pilgrimages. If we live our lives in that awareness, then such events can take on real meaning and importance. The sapiential books are an appeal, urging us never to let ourselves be beaten down by the problems and adversities of life, which are simply stumbling blocks on the road that can lead us to God.

To sum up once again, the wisdom thinking of the Hebrew people was very much like that of other peoples in antiquity. It is the voice of the people that speaks to us in this literature. As time went on, however, they more and more came to see God's revelation as relevant to the issues they were exploring in their wisdom thinking. The issues were intimately bound up with praxis, with God as origin and goal. Hence the sapiential books bear witness to the people's journey toward God —from the ground up, as it were.

This suggests an approach for today. People must think their own thoughts and express their own feelings. They must be allowed to find *their own* path to truth, to God. They must be given direction and guidance so that they may be able to discover God in and through *their own* life experiences. Truth cannot be imposed on people. We should never forget that the final syntheses of salvation history in the Old Testament, contained in the Book of Ecclesiasticus and the Book of Wisdom, were formulated on the basis of criteria that stemmed from the common people rather than the clergy. And that vision of salvation history crossed the threshold of the New Testament.

No loftier function could be found for the clergy today: Instead of using clerical categories, the clergy must try to ground revealed truth on the categories that the people themselves use to give orientation and direction to their lives.

Life and Death

As we have seen so far, the people represented in the sapiential books were characterized by a tendency to reflect on life. The accent was on sound sense and realism. It is not surprising, therefore, that they should be greatly preoccupied with the problems of suffering and death.

They confronted the problem of death with this sense of realism. Initially their ideal in life was to live to a ripe old age and to have a numerous progeny. Peaceful death in old age was life's crowning touch, and it caused no great problem in the people's minds. That kind of death was accepted as natural; it was part and parcel of life. The problem was premature death or death by violence, for this cut off a person's life before it had reached full term. It happened frequently enough. Cain killed Abel. Why? In chapter 1 we saw how the author of the Paradise account answered the question. He came from the circle of sages, and he maintained that violent death came into the world because humankind had already parted from God and gone off on its own.

As time went on, however, the fact of death itself became a problem. It called for some explanation. Why should we have to die when we have an indomitable will to live forever? This problem came into view because the people had been reflecting on life over a long period of time and their awareness had been sharpened by this reflection. The sage, schooled in this age-old reflection, began to look at reality more critically. He was no longer so readily willing to accept things as "natural." Moreover, serious reflection on the realities of life made it clear that even a happy death at the end of a long, full life could not be regarded as "natural," as the supreme fulfillment of a human being.

It is the book of Ecclesiastes, in particular, that marks a major step forward in this process of reflection. Looking at the world around him and reviewing all that had been said previously on the subject, even as we might do today, the author found that nothing was worth bothering about. Everything was "emptiness," and life was a farce (Eccl 1:2). To him life was a torment precisely because of the fact of death. Why should we kill ourselves with work if we have to die some day and leave our estate to another who might squander it? (Eccl 2:18–19): "As he came from the womb of mother earth, so must he return, naked as he came; all his toil produces nothing which he can take away with him" (Eccl 5:15).

The author subjects all the old answers to rigorous criticism. Nothing is of much use in life, and everything is worthless after death: "For man is a creature of chance and the beasts are creatures of chance, and one mischance awaits them all: death comes to both alike. All draw the same breath. Human beings have no advantage over beasts; for everything is emptiness. All go to the same place: All came from the dust, and to the dust all return. Who knows whether the spirit of the person goes upward or whether the spirit of the beast goes downward to the earth?" (Eccl 3:19–21). No one really knows what will happen after life is over.

In his reflection the author had raised dim hopes of some possible future after death. It would be nice if such a thing did exist. But then his bitter irony dashes to the ground any such hope. We yearn to live forever, but a barrier stands over against this yearning. Life has no real meaning, and death takes away all hope.

Here wisdom thinking comes up against an insoluble problem and confronts its own limitations.

Insofar as it allows itself to be guided by empirical observation in its conclusions, it cannot help but deduce that everything is ultimately absurd. But the sense of despair produced by the book of Ecclesiastes aroused in people a desire to know more about death and life. It created problems where none had seen any problem before.

Faith in God and Revelation of the Future

Thus people began to develop an even more critical outlook on reality, and certain problems were felt more deeply. What future can we look forward to? Death or life? God's promises to Abraham in the distant past had been framed in very concrete terms. He would be the father of a great people who would settle in a promised land and enjoy a blessed existence (Gn 12:1–3). That is what God had promised, and no one doubted that he would fulfill the promise. But life's realities indicated just the opposite. Instead of obtaining the future promised by God, the just were suffering ever greater oppression (Eccl 4:1–2); meanwhile, those who paid no heed to God were having a high time (Eccl 8:10). The situations of everyday life seemed to deny the justice of God and to speak out against his fidelity. The author of the book of Ecclesiastes seemed to be right. Why continue to believe in that God?

A conflict arose between faith and experience. It threatened to hurl people into total despair, calling everything into question: life, death, and even God.

The basic problem was that well-being here and now did not exhaust or fulfill our yearning for life and happiness, a yearning that had been stimulated by God's promise. Instead of bringing full life and complete happiness, God's promise brought frustration and ultimate disillusionment. This feeling found vivid expression in the book of Ecclesiastes. Yet this conflict between faith and experience forced people to look for new solutions and ultimately led them to achieve a new vision.

Nostalgic yearning for God and faith in God's fidelity and justice proved to be stronger than the seemingly contradictory nature of life. If God had made a promise, then this promise was somehow capable of being fulfilled. If the here and now seemed to deny that promise by virtue of its contradictory realities and the prospect of death, then God must somehow be stronger than death. In some way God must be able to maintain human life even through death. The bold thinking of faith led the Hebrews to break down the barrier of death and its negative influence on their hopes.

Faith in God's fidelity and strength helped the Hebrews to break out of the closed circle of their own reflections. It alerted them to the broader prospect of a life with God that would endure forever, a life supported by God's power and fidelity. Thus there arose a solid faith in the resurrection of the dead and a life with God after death. The revelation of these new truths did not come about by decree; it came about as a result of poignant reflection over the course of centuries, from the time of Abraham to the centuries just before the coming of Jesus Christ.

The first faint expressions of hope in some sort of life in God's presence after death are to be found in the Psalms (Pss 11:7; 17:15; 23:6; 27:4). But it is Psalm 73 that formulates this dawning realization most clearly: "When my heart was embittered I felt the pangs of envy, I would not understand, so brutish was I, I was a mere beast in thy sight, O God. Yet I am always with them, thou holdest my right hand; thou dost guide me by thy counsel and afterwards wilt receive me with glory. Whom have I in heaven but thee? And having thee, I desire nothing else on earth. Though heart and body fail, yet God is my possession forever. They who are far from thee are lost; thou dost destroy all who wantonly forsake thee. But my chief good is to be near thee, O God; I have chosen thee, Lord God, to be my refuge" (Ps 73:21–28).

Here we see faith courageously facing reality and not hesitating to affirm something that seems absurd: There is reason to hope because God will resurrect us from the dead. We find this truth clearly expressed in the first five chapters of the book of Wisdom. Here is an explicit passage: "But the souls of the just are in God's hand, and torment shall not touch them. In the eyes of foolish men they seemed to be dead; their departure was reckoned as defeat, and their going from us as disaster. But they are at peace, for though in the sight of men they may be punished, they have a sure hope of immortality; and after a little chastisement they will receive great blessings, because God has tested them and found them worthy to be his" (Wis 3:1–5). This realization represents a great achievement in the attempt to give proper direction to life.

Later, in the New Testament, Christ will complete this teaching concerning life after death and the victory of faith and hope. By virtue of faith, this enduring life is already present here and now. The future is already operative, transforming and resurrecting the world and humankind from the disastrous realities of evil and death. To believe in undying life is to believe in the possibility of the world being *renewed,* to wait for the new world to come out of the old world.

Final Considerations

In all this we find a profound human experience that is very much our own. We cannot manage to live wholly on our own. We all have to let our ego depend on someone else. That someone else will to some extent sustain us and make us feel that we are worthwhile and doing something useful. This feeling, in turn, will give impetus to our own energies.

Many depend on the power of friendship and human love. But when they reflect on the matter, they realize that the other person, the friend or lover, will die someday. Thus they will lose their source of support, because human friendship and love are not strong enough to overcome death.

Those who become aware of this limitation on friendship and love look elsewhere for some support that will help them to survive beyond death. (1) They look to their work, to the contribution they can make to the welfare of others. Their contribution will survive their death, and hence they will survive in some way; but their ego will melt into the collective life of the group and disappear. The ancient Egyptians thought like that, and so they invested much energy in constructing pyramids to ensure their survival after death. It certainly is some form of survival. (2) Others look to reasoned conclusions about life. Life, they say, is absurd and we must accept this absurdity. True human beings will accept the absurdity of life, live as best they can, and then disappear from existence at the moment of death. (3) Still others try to prolong their lives through their progeny. Their *name* will live on through their children. This, too, is a form of survival; but here again the personal self disappears. This form of survival—i.e., survival through procreation—degenerated into fertility cults among the ancient Canaanites in Palestine.

All these attempts to prolong the life of the self

and give meaning to existence failed to give lasting satisfaction. The fact was that the personal self would eventually die and disappear. Biblical thought broke out of this closed circle of reflection concerning survival. A *Voice* freely chooses to speak to us, a Voice that comes from a realm of life that is not subject to death. It stands outside the closed circle of life and death in which we dwell. This loving Voice establishes a dialogue with us, summoning each of us by name and alerting us to new possibilities. We sense the presence of a force that can now keep us alive and restore us to life after death.

This divine force of love and friendship calls us by name and confers value on us. It will remain operative forever, because love truly lived goes on forever. We have entered into dialogue with God, who summons us to go on living. Our will to live is aroused and given impetus by the love of God; we want to survive death and go on living forever. This new desire is later given confirmation in the resurrection of Jesus Christ. It is this friendship and love that confers eternal value on all human friendship and love. Nothing is lost. Everything is an expression of the faith and hope that enables us to live forever.

9

Job: The Drama of Us All

The drama is about to begin. The audience in the hall grows silent. But the curtain stays down, and instead a narrator steps out to introduce the subject at hand. He will acquaint the audience with the subject that is to be explored and debated in the drama itself. It is a concrete problem dealing with human beings and their destiny.

The Narrator's Role

The narrator begins: "There lived in the land of Uz a man of blameless and upright life named Job, who feared God and set his face against wrongdoing" (Jb 1:1). This man Job was upright, wealthy, well-known, prosperous and happy (Jb 1:2–5).

Now the narrator takes us behind the scenes to where human destiny is discussed and decided. We are allowed to listen to a conversation that determines what will happen in a person's life, the kind of conversation that lies beyond the range of our ordinary human hearing. We are present at a meeting in heaven where God determines the lot of people. Satan is a participant in this particular discussion. He is the "devil's advocate" in the testing of humanity, the prosecutor who lays bare our faults before God.

At this particular meeting God approaches Satan and calls his attention to the exemplary life of Job: "A man of blameless and upright life, who fears God and sets his face against wrongdoing" (Jb 1:8). Satan does not accept that verdict, maintaining that Job's supposed integrity is due to the fact that he is blessed and prosperous: "Has not Job good reason to be God-fearing? Have you not hedged him round on every side with your protection, him and his family and all his possessions? Whatever he does you have blessed . . . " (Jb 1:9–10). Job's goodness is merely a superficial pose, claims Satan: "But stretch out your hand and touch all that he has, and then he will curse you to your face" (Jb 1:11).

God accepts the challenge: "So be it. All that he has is in your hands" (Jb 1:12). Satan is given permission to test Job's honesty and uprightness. He can do whatever he wants to Job, but he cannot touch Job's person. Suddenly, without Job knowing why, one disaster after another falls upon him. He loses everything, including his children; he and his wife are left desolate and alone (Jb 1:13–19).

It is too much to bear! In despair Job rends his garments and cries out: "Naked I came from the womb, naked I shall return where I came" (Jb 1:21). But even with all that has befallen him, Job will not curse God. He "did not charge God with unreason" (Jb 1:22). Instead he reacts with resignation: "The Lord gives and the Lord takes away; blessed be the name of the Lord" (Jb 1:21).

When the heavenly court meets again, God tries to show Satan that he has erred in his judgment of Job (Jb 2:1–3). Job is virtue incarnate; his piety is not a façade. But Satan is not convinced: "There is nothing the man will grudge to save himself. But stretch out your hand and touch his bone and his flesh, and see if he will not curse you to your face" (Jb 2:4–5). God again accepts the challenge and gives Satan permission to strike Job: "So be it. He is in your hands" (Jb 2:6). The only restriction is that Satan may not kill Job.

Suddenly, without knowing why, Job is stricken with leprosy and becomes a terrible sight. He has only a piece of broken pottery to use for scratching his sores, and he goes to sit on a pile of ashes (Jb 2:7–8). Even his wife wants nothing to do with him because she cannot stand his fetid breath alongside her in bed (Jb 19:17). She even tries to get him to rebel against God, for the Lord has certainly not been kind to Job: "Are you still unshaken in your integrity? Curse God and die!" (Jb 2:9). But Job will not listen to such talk: "You talk as any wicked fool of a woman might talk. If we accept good from God, shall we not accept evil?" (Jb 2:10). He refuses to rebel against God.

So Job has lost everything. His suffering is so great that one can hardly imagine it. What is worse, he himself does not know why he is being subjected to such suffering. He has not been privy to the meetings in heaven at which his fate has been decided. He simply suffers the consequences of the decisions made there. And in the opinion of his contemporaries, there was only one explanation for such terrible suffering: It was a punishment from God! Job must be a terrible sinner!

Three friends hear of the misfortunes that have befallen Job. They come from afar to share his suffering, offer him some consolation, and display their sympathy (Jb 2:11). Job is so changed that they hardly recognize him (Jb 2:12). His plight overwhelms them. Speechless, they sit down to bemoan his plight. For "seven days and seven nights" they did not say a word, for they saw "that his suffering was very great" (Jb 2:13).

The suffering of the just man: Who can explain it? That is the problem that will be discussed in the drama. The narrator has presented the audience with a concrete case, one of countless such cases. He disappears now from the stage and the curtain slowly rises.

The Question of Suffering

Silence has reigned for seven days and seven nights. As the curtain opens we see Job in his pile of ashes and his friends close by. His silent suffering reaches down through the long centuries into our own hearts. Unable to explain such suffering, we sit silently and wait, alongside Job and his three friends.

Suddenly a terrible cry pierces the silence. It is a bitter complaint. The audience shudders, but is pleased at the same time. Job has the guts to voice his complaint, to shout to the four winds. He is willing to give expression to the feelings of the just person who suffers without knowing why: "Perish the day when I was born and the night which said, 'A man is conceived'! May that day turn to darkness; may God above not look for it, nor light of dawn shine on it. . . . Why was I not still-born, why did I not die when I came out of the womb? Why was I ever laid on my mother's knees or put to suck at her breasts? For then I should be lying in the quiet grave, asleep in death, at rest. . . . Why should the sufferer be born to see the light? Why is life given to men who find it so bitter? . . . There is no peace of mind nor quiet for me; I chafe in torment and have no rest" (Jb 3:3–4, 11–13, 20, 26).

Thus Job initiates the debate, laying the problem right on the table. A man has chosen to seek the meaning of life, the reason for his suffering and torment. A problem that confronts us all is laid bare on the stage in the person of Job, the central character in the drama that will unfold before us. We are born without asking to be born, and there are people waiting to receive us. We are brought into life only to suffer and die senselessly, without knowing the reason for either life or suffering or death.

On the stage we also see the various efforts we make to explain the reason for suffering. They are embodied in Job's three friends, and in the young man who will show up later (Jb 32–37). None of the characters in the drama knows about the deliberations in heaven or the reason for what has happened to Job. Like the audience, like us, they have brought along their own sufferings and see them vividly imprinted on Job. Like us, they keep trying to find some explanation that will make life more tolerable. Like us, they engage in every sort of rationalization.

Job's three friends are on the side of the audience insofar as they embody the traditional explanations that are offered for the sufferings we encounter in life. But the audience must also admire the courage of Job, who is bold enough to challenge what most regard as sacrosanct. Starting from his own life experience, Job is willing to confront long-held traditions and challenge age-old ways of thinking. Why? Because in their attempt to defend God they tell lies about human life (Jb 13:7–8).

As the drama unfolds, the audience will be able to

hear and evaluate the arguments and consoling words offered to Job. We will see to what extent they explain suffering and stand up against the realistic, anguished awareness of a suffering man like Job. His three friends will voice and defend the arguments that people are wont to offer. They will not allow a suffering and disillusioned individual to undermine the solid foundations of traditional piety that had been their source of security in life. Which will win here—tradition or personal conscience?

The dialogue between Job and his friends is one that goes on inside all of us when we are confronted with suffering. It is the dialogue that goes on between the older generation and the younger generation, between those who cling to what has been handed down by tradition and those who find such traditional explanations no answer to the problems and questions raised by their own experiences.

The Existential Problem in the Book of Job

For a long time the cultural situation of the Hebrew people had been tribal and pastoral. Everything belonged to everyone, and all the people shared a common lot. All were well off or all suffered poverty, and hence there was a strong feeling of group solidarity. In that cultural context it seemed quite natural that one person should suffer because of the evil committed by another (Jos

7:1–26). There was even a proverb to that effect: "The fathers have eaten sour grapes, and the children's teeth are set on edge" (Ez 18:2). At this point no one knew anything about the future that lay beyond death. It was felt that all would share the same lot, whether they were good or evil in life (Eccl 9:1–2). All would go down to a shadowy existence in a place called *sheol*.

Living in this cultural context, the people tried to express their faith in a personal God by offering some explanation for suffering. God was just. He rewarded the good and punished the evil. Hence evil was to be regarded as a punishment inflicted by God. If a good person was faced with suffering, then that suffering must be a punishment for sins committed by others. If a person was enjoying happiness and prosperity, that must be a reward for his own goodness or the goodness of others. There was no thought at this point of reward or punishment after death. This explanation satisfied the nomadic Hebrew people and resolved the problem of the suffering inflicted on the just person. It fit well into the context of their pastoral culture and gave them a satisfactory idea of God and his justice.

The transition from pastoral life to a settled agricultural society brought profound changes to the Hebrew people. A sense of personal awareness and individual conscience grew. They now lived in settled towns and cities where each person cultivated his own field or engaged in trade. The older notion of group solidarity in good and evil faded away. It came to be felt that each person got what he earned, that results were the product of personal work and effort. It was no longer tolerable to think that one person should suffer for the evil committed by another person. The prophet Ezekiel sought to explain God's justice in this new cultural framework (Ez 18:2 ff.): One could not maintain that God would punish the children for their parents' sins; each individual would get his due from God, otherwise God would be unjust.

But notice what happened at this point. The people attempted to deal with the new cultural data in terms of their old criteria. Evil was a punishment from God. If a person was suffering, and if such suffering was not a punishment inflicted on him because of the sins of others, then only one explanation remained: *The person was suffering because he himself was a sinner!* Wealth and happiness were tokens of God's reward for goodness; the prosperous man must also be a just man. Poverty and unhappiness were tokens of divine punishment for wickedness; *the poor man must also be a sinner*. In this way Hebrew theology tried to salvage the data of tradition regarding God's justice. Job was right. In trying to defend God, people were telling lies about life (Jb 13:7–8).

That is the backdrop for the existential problem which gave rise to the book of Job and which is discussed in it. It gives vivid expression to the anguish of a suffering human being. Tradition, the whole structure of Hebrew societal life and its prevailing outlook, and even Job himself insofar as he was a product of that society, said that Job must be a terrible sinner rejected by God, that the severity of his sufferings attested to the seriousness of his sin. But on the other hand Job's conscience told him that he was innocent (Jb 6:29). God was cruel and unjust to treat him that way (Jb 30:21). It was a source of keen anguish to find oneself spurned by Someone whom one had tried to love and serve faithfully (Jb 16:17).

God, it seemed, had withdrawn from Job. Job racked his brain and examined his conscience, but he could not find any indication that he had offended God in any way (Jb 27:5–6; 31:1–40). Job could only wonder why "the arrows of the Almighty find their mark in me" (Jb 6:4). Feelings of revolt against God welled up in his heart (Jb 23:2). Yet at the same time Job believed that God was just, more just than human beings. So there must be some reason why God was punishing him this way and treating him as an enemy (Jb 19:11). Tradition said one thing, his conscience another. Which side was right: God, as tradition and Job had always conceived him, or Job's conscience? How could one be loyal to God and to his own conscience at the same time? This is the root question raised by the book of Job.

The Hebrew people had fallen on evil days.

Crises and calamities multiplied day by day. This unfortunate situation came to a head in a personal crisis for the person who wrote the book of Job. The character of Job gives expression to feelings that were stirring in the hearts of all the Hebrew people. Hence the book of Job was a powerful stimulus to consciousness-raising among them.

Invitation to Participation

The way the drama is set up, Job and his friends do not know what the audience knows. They have not been clued in by the narrator. So the audience has a criterion for judging and evaluating the correctness of the arguments that will be put forth by various characters in the drama. In this dramatization, Job represents *the new awareness of personal conscience* that is emerging among the Hebrew people; his friends represent *tradition and the attempt to defend its inherited arguments and values.*

Those in the audience will find themselves on both sides of the fence in the ensuing discussion, because both Job and his friends voice feelings shared by the listeners. Job's friends represent the audience inasmuch as we all have a desire to follow the age-old ways of thinking, thus avoiding new problems and challenges. Job is on the side of the public inasmuch as he is courageous enough to speak out against things we all would like to see criticized. But he is the enemy of the public because he threatens to demolish the supporting framework of tradition and the peace of mind it affords us; he unmasks the false and spurious reasoning behind which we hide. Job's friends are on the side of the audience when they defend tradition. They are enemies of the audience when they seek to dominate personal awareness and impede its solid growth, when they are willing to "assail an orphan" and gang up on a friend in the name of God and tradition (Jb 6:27).

The discussion between Job and his friends proceeds slowly. It reveals humankind as it truly is: fragile yet self-reliant, weak yet proud, ignorant yet knowledgeable, forsaken yet sure-footed.

Job is in torment because tradition suggests that his suffering is the product of personal sinfulness. Yet his own conscience tells him that he has not committed any sin which merits such punishment. In this case the reader of the book of Job, the person watching the unfolding drama, knows that the traditional opinion is not applicable. But Job does not know that, nor do his three friends. To apply the criterion of tradition in a hard and fast way is the height of injustice, the worst lie imaginable.

But how is one to dismantle the arguments of tradition? This is the question tackled by the author in his drama. Operating on the data of his own experience and conscience, Job will attempt to tear down the arguments of tradition. He cannot look to any other person or even to the structure of his

society for defense. His only defense is the voice of
his own conscience. Yet, despite these odds, personal conscience gains the upper hand as the debate advances. It reduces the arguments of tradition
to dust and ashes (Jb 13:12), hot air (Jb 16:3), and
treachery (Jb 6:15–18). Job makes his bold challenge:
"Tell me plainly, and I will listen in silence; show
me where I have erred" (Jb 6:24). He will not be
talked down to: "No doubt you are perfect men and
absolute wisdom is yours! But I have sense as well
as you; in nothing do I fall short of you; what gifts
indeed have you that others have not?" (Jb 12:2–3).

An Erroneous Conception of God

The author is not content merely to tear apart the
arguments of tradition. The basic problem is a
deeper one. It is not enough to say what things are
not. Mere refutation of other people's arguments
will not provide a way out of the dilemma. Job's real
conflict is not with his friends or with tradition. It is
with God himself: "What you know, I also know; in
nothing do I fall short of you. But for my part I
would speak with the Almighty and am ready to
argue with God" (Jb 13:2–3). Job is ready to go all
the way: "You like fools are smearing truth with
your falsehoods, stitching a patchwork of lies, one
and all. Ah, if you would only be silent and let
silence be your wisdom! . . . Is it on God's behalf
that you speak so wickedly, or in his defense that

you allege what is false? Must you take God's part, or put his case for him? . . . Be silent, leave me to speak my mind, and let what may come upon me! I will put my neck in the noose and take my life in my hands. If he would slay me, I should not hesitate; I should still argue my cause to his face. This at least assures my success, that no godless man may appear before him" (Jb 13:4–5, 7–8, 13–16).

And so Job moves on to argue with God himself: "Take thy heavy hand clean away from me and let not the fear of thee strike me with dread. Then summon me, and I will answer; or I will speak first, and do thou answer me. How many iniquities and sins are laid to my charge?" (Jb 13:21–23). Before he hurled down this challenge Job had told his friends: "Be sure of this: Once I have stated my case I know that I shall be acquitted" (Jb 13:18).

The drama is a kind of jury trial. God and man are brought into court to settle their differences. Job wants to make a case against God, to present his own defense against God's way of dealing with him (Jb 23:4); and he is sure that he will be cleared by his defense (Jb 23:7). But the opinions of Job's three friends, both pro and con, will not do. It is God himself who must decide between God and man (Jb 16:21). In taking this stance, Job detaches himself from his friends, from society, and from everything that had determined his life up to this point. He sets out alone on a bold new path. He simply must find some solution to the problem that now weighs upon him. It is an authentic human problem, a problem concerning God's presence in our lives.

God accepts Job's proposal, and he delivers a long discourse about divine wisdom and its role in the vast universe (Jb 38–41). Job had questioned God and expounded his own problem in life. Now God questions Job: "Brace yourself and stand up like a man; I will ask questions, and you shall answer" (Jb 38:3). He then goes on to describe the marvels of the universe in all their mysteriousness. Job cannot explain or even know them, but they all have meaning in the design of God's wisdom.

At the end of God's discourse, Job sees the whole problem in a new light: "I knew of thee then only *by report*, but now *I see thee with my own eyes*. Therefore I melt away; I repent in dust and ashes" (Jb 42:5–6). An old image of God, one transmitted from the past *by report*, crumbles away. A whole new image of God comes to life in Job's mind, an image based on his own personal experience. A new light has dawned on the horizon of Job's life, and peace and tranquility return to him. The problem in life does not come from God but from the mistaken image of God that traditional report had imprinted on Job's mind. Through his personal encounter with God, Job was able to rid himself of the old image and discover a new vision for himself and others.

The author does not tell us exactly what solution Job found. But he does offer the reader all the elements and clues he needs to go through the same process as Job and arrive at the same conclusion that Job reached. This is the dramatic technique that typifies the sapiential writers. They are not interested in teaching some abstract solution. They want to get the readers to participate in the search for a solution, to discover the truth for themselves. The readers must do their own reflecting to see if they can identify with Job and discover for themselves what Job himself discovered.

Finally the curtain descends. The narrator returns and pronounces the final verdict: Job's friends lost the debate. God's verdict is: "I am angry with you . . . because you have not spoken as you ought about me, as my servant Job has done" (Jb 42:7). In using tired old arguments to defend a no longer defensible viewpoint, they became the people on trial. They are in the wrong and must beg pardon of Job. For he had the courage to confront God, reality, and tradition, relying solely on the testimony of his own conscience (Jb 42:7–9). The narrator ends by saying that prosperity returned to Job, indicating that Job found God and interior peace once again (Jb 42:10–17).

Conclusion

The drama presented in the book of Job represents the actual experience of some Hebrew. He shares with his readers his own itinerary, his own way of confronting the mystery of suffering.

Perhaps the readers would find this useful as well. Hoary outlooks inherited from tradition must be discarded when they can no longer account for reality. A new sense of awareness must be developed.

Job and his friends represent humanity journeying the road of life, arguing about the sufferings that bow them down. Thus we have perennial conflict between revelation and reality, between the thoughts enshrined in an age-old culture and the happenings that confront individuals in their own lifetimes. Today the human conscience is again on the stage, sitting on a pile of ashes, alienated in a thousand different ways, forced into debate with traditional views. The general public is privy to the drama through the news media and the television set. The debate proceeds slowly with many twists and turns, but human awareness and personal conscience are getting the upper hand.

In the last analysis, it was not Job's three friends but Job himself who defended and preserved the authentic value of tradition. It was he who broke ground for a new encounter with God, who got beyond the barrier erected by his three friends and their traditional schemas. The book of Job brought down a whole theology and cleared the ground for something new. It did not solve the problem once and for all, but that was not its intention. It simply wanted to clear away an obstacle that was preventing further progress, and it succeeded admirably.

Job's three friends were left with the shell of tradition after Job himself managed to dig out the real meat.

The book of Job shows us that the people of God must engage in criticism and challenging confrontation. Job was not afraid to raise questions when he realized that his conscience could not accept the traditional position. To rule out the possibility of critical questioning is to dig a grave for the very position we are trying to defend against criticism. When the human conscience is not permitted to express itself, then it cannot help but speak out bluntly: "Be silent, leave me to speak my mind. What you know I also know" (Jb 13:13,2). Job's three friends, and their descendants living today, must remember that God acquitted Job. He had spoken rightly of God though they thought he was in error.

The book of Job represents a most significant and truly human breakthrough. The author, a member of the chosen people, uses the figure of a legendary character known as Job to describe his own experience with God. This legendary character was an internationally known figure, not a member of the Hebrew nation. It is as if a modern Christian were to describe his personal experience with Christ in terms of a figure like Gandhi, who is already legendary.

The book of Job typifies the attitude of the sapiential writers toward life. Their point of departure is

our conscious awareness, our yearning not to be
ground under by life. Life and its problems are their
chief concern. Their approach is not to impose some
solution on the readers but to get them thinking, to
have them discover their own way. The distin-
guishing mark of these writers is realism, and their
discussions take place in the intimate circle of close
friends. On stage, in this particular case, we find
Job, his three friends, and later a young man named
Elihu. It is a meeting of *wise men* to discuss the
problems of life, and such meetings are common-
place around the world.

The book of Job is hard to understand because its
literary idiom is complex and alien to us. But the
problem under discussion was never more pertinent. Despite the problems of communication on
the literary level, the discussion and its message
come across loud and clear.

10

The Psalms: A Summary
of the Old Testament

The Psalms are almost a summary of the entire Old Testament, not in the sense that they contain a little bit of everything but in the sense that they present the most basic attitude of the Old Testament in every conceivable form. When people are disposed to live their lives as a response to God's summons, then their lives should be characterized by a particular attitude or outlook. They must be ready to move ahead with a sense of certainty and to hold the reins of history in their hands. This attitude pervades the Psalms.

Difficulties in Praying the Psalms

The Psalms portray God as Someone who makes his presence known at any given moment. He is in direct communication with human beings. He intervenes at critical moments in life, helps the Hebrews to win battles, cures illness, guides people's footsteps, and even alters the natural course of events in order to carry out his plan. But today God does not seem to be around. His activity is not within the bounds of empirical observation. For people today, and particularly for city dwellers, God is no longer a natural fact of life. Instead he has become an unnecessary hypothesis. Atheism is a practical attitude which more and more people accept without question. The world of the Old Testament and the world of today are very different ones. It seems impossible to recite the Psalms and then go out and live life earnestly in today's world.

Praying itself is a difficult project. It is not easy to have recourse to Someone who remains invisible. Contact with other human beings is difficult enough. It takes real effort to open up to another person, to exclude other stimuli and focus our attention on the person to whom we are talking. Most of our conversations are superficial chatter rather than dialogue. How much more difficult it is to talk to Someone who is invisible.

Moreover, the Psalms come to us as ancient prayers from a very different cultural milieu. Their idiom is alien to us, their symbols and imagery quite different from those we are used to today. We are unfamiliar with the historical events to which they allude, with the life situation of those who formulated them. Thus it is not easy for us to identify with the Psalms, to recognize our own selves and our historical circumstances in them.

Finally, some of the Psalms seem far from perfect as prayers. Some express desires for violent and hate-filled revenge. How indeed can we recite such imperfect prayers today?

The Psalms as Representative Prayers

The Psalms should not be regarded as the most perfect form or expression of prayer. There are excellent Psalms and imperfect ones, Psalms that are literary masterpieces and Psalms that are little more than plagiarisms.

Nor should the Psalms be viewed as a monolithic block that dropped from heaven one day. The book of Psalms was not composed in a day. It was fashioned over a long period of time. Composition probably began in the time of King David (around 1000 B.C.) and was completed around 300 B.C. Even after the book of Psalms was completed, the original wellspring of such prayers did not dry up. Several facts reveal this to be true: (1) In the Greek translation of the Old Testament (called the Septuagint), we find fourteen Psalms or "odes" that are not in the original Hebrew text. (2) In the Dead Sea Scrolls, which were discovered betweeen 1947 and 1956 but date back to somewhere around 100 B.C., we find a large number of Psalms that are not contained in the biblical book of Psalms. (3) In many other sections of the Bible, including the historical, the sapiential, and the prophetical writings, we find prayers and psalms which are not recorded in the book of Psalms itself.

Thus the book of Psalms contains only some of the prayers that were recited by the Hebrew people. It is a limited anthology, a sample of the way people prayed and sang to God. It is part of a centuries-old movement of prayer, and it does not claim to hold a monopoly over the nation's prayer life. It does not rule out other prayers. Instead it is intended to stimulate prayer and carry on a long tradition. Most important is not the Psalms themselves but the long-standing prayer movement from which they arose and to which they try to give further impetus.

The Psalms are a reflection of humankind's slow ascent toward God over the centuries, and our progressive liberation through this contact with God. They preserve both the perfections and the imperfections connected with that ascent.

The imperfections (the sentiments of hatred, self-sufficiency, and vengeance, for example) tend to diminish over the course of time. They are more evident in the older Psalms. The Psalms bear witness to humankind's earnest effort to be loyal to God and itself. They are prayers of people like ourselves, people journeying toward the goal established for us by God.

The imperfections show us that God is willing to accept the prayers of which we are capable. Otherwise God would not have inspired them. The important thing is that the prayer be sincere.

The Origin of the Book of Psalms

The book of Psalms is an artificial collection of 150 Psalms, brought together in one book for liturgical purposes. Its Hebrew title is *Sefer Tehillim*, which means "Book of Hymns." Yet the explanatory titles for the individual Psalms, which are not translated in all English versions, indicate that only one Psalm is a *Tehila*, a "hymn": Psalm 145. The more frequent title for the collection is the "Book of Psalms." The word "psalm" (*Mismor* in Hebrew) indicates a particular way of singing or chanting. Today we talk about ballads, blues, country and western, and rock songs. The ancient Hebrews talked about hymns (*tehillim*), psalms (*mismor*), canticles (*shirim*), and so forth.

If you are reading an English translation with the Hebrew titles included, you will notice a certain element of confusion. One title may indicate that the Psalm in question is a "hymn"; another title may indicate that the Psalm in question is a "Psalm." But the fact is that the book of Psalms contains all sorts of chants and prayers: hymns, psalms, canticles, lamentations, and so forth. Evidently the Hebrews did not find it easy to classify the content of the materials in the book of Psalms, since those materials were quite diverse in their origin. It is always difficult to classify the complicated features of *life* under a neat title.

There is nothing sacred or exhaustive about the

number of Psalms in our present book of Psalms. There we find 150 Psalms, which was a nice round number for the anthology. We, too, try to get a representative number of songs and hymns into our liturgical hymnbooks.

Various collections of chants and prayers were in existence before the book of Psalms was put together, just as we have various collections of hymns today. The Hebrews had songs to be sung on pilgrimages, and we note that some Psalms are called "songs of ascent" (Pss 120–134). Others were meant to be sung during the paschal meal, and they are referred to as *hallel* or "Alleluia" songs (Pss 105–107, 111–118, 135–136, 146–150). The Hebrews also had collections by various authors, just as we have records and song books by different entertainers today. At the end of Psalm 72 we find this notation: "Here end the prayers of David, Son of Jesse." Other Psalms are attributed to Moses, Solomon, and the Sons of Korah.

Eventually an attempt was made to put together a definitive or standard anthology of the songs and chants on the market. They were culled from every available source, which explains why we find some repetition: compare Psalm 14 and Psalm 53, Psalm 40:13–17 and Psalm 70. Some Psalms existed in more than one collection with slight textual variations, and others were added without too much organization in mind. The biblical text says that the prayers of David end with Psalm 72, but in fact some subsequent Psalms are also attributed to him.

The composer of the final edition divided the Psalms into five basic collections or divisions. He ends each division with a similar refrain: "Blessed be the Lord the God of Israel from everlasting to everlasting; and let all the people say 'Amen' " (Ps 106:48; also see the end verse of Psalms 41, 73, and 89). Psalm 150, the final one, is an elaboration of this basic proclamation.

Thus the background and history of the psalter reveals its roots in the life of the Hebrew people. The Psalms focus and channel the living concerns of God's people, and hence they were much publicized and widely known.

Singing the Psalms

If we want to appreciate the place that the Psalms held in the life of the Hebrew people, we must also know something of the way they were recited or sung. Here again their approach was very much like ours today.

Many Psalms have brief explanatory titles which indicate their origin and the way in which they were to be sung. Many had instrumental accompaniment. Psalm 150 mentions some of these instruments. They were obviously instruments used for popular music, just as we use the guitar, banjo, and fiddle for our folk music. The people often joined in with a simple phrase or verse such as "Amen" or "Alleluia." "Amen" is equivalent to "So be it" or "That's right!" "Alleluia" means "praise to

Yahweh." Some of the Psalms are equivalent to our litanies. Instead of saying "Pray for us" the Hebrews responded *ci ad olam hesdo,* which means "his love endures forever" (Ps 136). At times the people would simply join in with a short rhythmic chant—reiterating the name Yahweh, for example (1 Chr 29:20).

The Hebrews often adopted the melody of some popular song for a given Psalm, just as we adapt old melodies to new lyrics today. Thus Psalm 22 is to be sung to the tune of "The Hind of the Dawn." The melody of another tune, "Do Not Destroy," is to be used for Psalms 57, 58, and 59 (see also the explanatory titles for Pss 18, 45, 46, 53, 56, 60, 69, 75, 80, 81, and 84).

Some of the titles also give directions to the chorus or choir. Certain Psalms are to be started by "the leader" (Pss 14, 21, 31). Psalm 88 is to be sung "as a lament." Psalm 7 is to be sung "as a plaintive song."

All these little pieces of information in the book of Psalms attest to the popular origin of the Psalms themselves.

The Author of the Psalms

According to the Hebrew text of the Psalms, seventy-three were composed by David, twelve by Asaph, eleven by the Sons of Korah, one by

Heman, one by Ethan, one by Moses, a few by Solomon, and thirty-five by anonymous authors. The Greek translation attributes eighty-five Psalms to David.

The frequent attribution of individual Psalms to David and the attribution of the whole book of Psalms to him is more a theological datum than a historical one. There is no reason to deny that David composed many Psalms, but he certainly did not compose all of them. But just as Moses stands at the origin of Hebrew legislation and Solomon at the origin of Hebrew wisdom thinking, so David stands at the origin of the Hebrew prayer movement. He was a striking personage whose sincere piety gave great impetus to the people's prayer life. To attribute the authorship of a Psalm to David was to give it official status in the liturgical life of the nation and to underline its value for the people's prayer life.

Modern Interpretation of the Psalms

The Psalms have been recited throughout the history of the Church, and many have tried to explain them and interpret them for the Christian people. One of the most famous of these commentators was Saint Augustine. His concern was to interpret the Psalms in such a way that the people of his own day (fourth century A.D.) could see them as a reflection of their own faith and life circumstances. He took the needs of his contemporaries as his point of departure and tried to offer a solid response to them.

As time went on, however, there developed a separation between the existential situation and the life of faith. The Psalms were relegated to the sidelines of life; they were to nourish a faith that often was out of touch with experience. Scriptural exegesis then sought new approaches to address this problem and re-establish a link between faith, prayer life, and everyday living. Most of the time, however, the Psalms were treated and presented as a monolithic block of homogeneous material.

Then a German exegete entered the picture. Herman Gunkel applied the critical notion of "literary genres" to the Psalms and tried to see how the Psalms had fit into the life of the Hebrew people. He managed to pinpoint the varied strands in the Psalms and trace them back to the diverse aspects of the nation's life. Using the notion of literary genres, he divided the Psalms up into different types of prayer: hymns, laments, petitions, meditated history, and so forth. Each type presupposed some specific milieu in which it grew.

Gunkel's work marked an important step forward, for now the Psalms could be seen as reflections of the people's life and its various aspects. But important and valuable as such research is, we simply cannot stop there. We must untangle the various threads, but that in itself does not get us back to the ultimate source. One seemingly curious thing, for example, is the fact that exegetes and commentators often disagree in their classifications of a given Psalm. Why? In my opinion, it is because life itself does not respect our neat divisions and classifications. We must therefore go beyond the literary genres if we wish to find the wellspring of the Psalms.

That source is closer to us than we might think. It is our own lives as human beings, illuminated by the summons of a God who calls out to us. As we probe the Psalms we discover life, the same life that we are living today. In the Psalms we discover something of ourselves and our life; they thus become authentic expressions of what is going on in our own minds and hearts. Viewed from this perspective, the Psalms present us with life in all its rawness, with life as it wells up from inside us. Life forces us to ask questions, to experience its joys and sorrows and anxieties, to consciously feel disquiet and uneasiness. We are forced to echo the words of Saint Augustine: "You have made us for yourself, O God, and our hearts will not rest until they rest in thee."

In this way the Psalms can achieve the purpose for which they were inspired. They can help us to discover who we are and what our true responsibility is. Shaking us out of our comfortable ease, they can give us new hope and keep us moving in the direction God wants us to go. They are a faithful mirror of life, a critical reflection of our true identity.

Difficulty in Interpreting the Psalms

At the root of the difficulties mentioned earlier is the most serious problem that faces us in trying to recite the Psalms. For reasons already mentioned, the Psalms lie outside the bounds of our own interests. They seem to have nothing to say of our lives. Everything is different: the problems, the language, the culture, the historical situation. Since there is no common bond of shared experience, all the various interpretations and explanations of the Psalms seem to fall into a void. They just do not seem to have any real value for us. They leave us in the dark about ourselves because they do not really speak to us; and hence they also leave us in the dark about God, who supposedly is speaking to us through them.

This difficulty, however, is based on a mistake we ourselves make. First, we do not probe deeply enough into our own lives; hence we cannot detect the pulse that throbs through the Psalms. Second, we do not try hard enough to deepen our knowledge of the Psalms; hence we do not come to see human life itself as the true source of all those prayers. If we probed deeply enough into our own lives and into the Psalms, we would soon discover that the two realities are interconnected and go back to the same source: people seeking meaning in life, people confronted with the problem of the Absolute as it is reflected in the many and varied problems of everyday life.

We cannot get at the root of the Psalms and pray them as our own unless and until we arrive at the realization that we have the same root deep inside ourselves. Strange as they may seem to us, the Psalms grew out of the same kind of situations and experiences that we are confronted with today. We share the same feelings: joy, gratitude, sadness, despair, anguish, and frustration. We must face the same problems: war, betrayal, lack of understanding, pain, and suffering. We, too, experience the seeming contradictions of life and its lack of meaning. If people have not faced up to such situations in their own lives, then they will find it very difficult to pray the Psalms as their own.

Hence if we are to interpret and pray the Psalms correctly, we must face up to one major task. We must live our own lives here and now in all the scope and depth that true living entails. We must face the problems and feelings of life openly and completely. This is what will unite us across the distance of time and space with the authors of the Psalms. Only then will the Psalms become an authentic expression of our own lives, regaining their full force as a human discourse directed to God. Only then will they be able to stimulate us to create new prayers of our own. Only then will we be able to pick up and continue the human search for God which finds such eloquent expression in the Psalms: "All the time that I dwelt among men who hated peace, I sought peace" (Ps 120).

Our Search for God

Today it seems to many people that God has become superfluous. They still believe that God exists, but they cannot determine his relevance to human life. Of what use is God? What value or meaning does God have in terms of concrete living?

We find the same problem expressed in the Bible. The Hebrew people believed in God's existence, but his presence was hard to discover: "How long, O Lord, wilt thou quite forget me? How long wilt thou hide thy face from me?" (Ps 13:1). The Hebrews felt abandoned: "But now thou hast rejected and humbled us. . . . Thou hast sold thy people for next to nothing and had no profit from the sale" (Ps 44:9, 12). The state of abandonment to which they were reduced at times seemed to prove that God was absent. It gave rise to terrible crises of faith: "I will say to God my rock, 'Why hast thou forgotten me?' Why must I go like a mourner. . . . My enemies taunt me, jeering at my misfortunes; 'Where is your God?' they ask me all day long" (Ps 42:9–10). Like many people today, the ancient Hebrews often felt that they did not know what to tell their children about God.

"Where is your God?" (Pss 42:3, 10; 79:10; 115:2).
That was an ever recurring question, and the Hebrews, like us, often found it hard to answer. To have
a God and yet not be able to point him out is a
disturbing situation. It prompts a person to rebel.
After all, what sort of a God is that?

The Bible is nothing else but a vivid response to
that question, a question that is still ours today.
Leaving aside the theoretical problem, many people today focus on the practical issue of God's significance in their own lives. The traditional God-concept does not seem to offer any substantive content for everyday life. God is considered irrelevant,
an opiate preventing people from making progress
and alienating them from the world. God is dead!
Long live man!

If we read the Psalms, however, we soon realize
that this is an old problem. Even then people had
the same thoughts: "What does God know? The
Most High neither knows nor cares" (Ps 73:11).
Many come to the conclusion that "there is no God"
(Ps 14:1). And so they conspire against God and his
people: "Let us break their fetters, . . . let us throw
off their chains" (Ps 2:3). They become cocksure:
"Our tongue can win the day. Words are our ally;
who can master us?" (Ps 12:4). Everyone looks out
for himself and gets along the best he can (Ps
11:1–2).

Indeed life does seem easier without God. We are
freed from useless anxiety and are more capable of
unhindered progress and growth. People say God

neither knows nor cares, "yet still they prosper, and rogues amass great wealth" (Ps 73:12). It is those who try to believe in God that seem to suffer most, and they are sorely tempted to rid themselves of the burden: "So it was all in vain that I kept my heart pure and washed my hands in innocence. For all day long I suffer torment and am punished every morning" (Ps 73:13–14). Yet something tells the faithful believers that this line of thinking will not solve anything, that it is mere evasion: "Yet had I let myself talk on in this fashion, I should have betrayed the family of God" (Ps 73:15). They choose to take on the contradictory burden of God, to reject the easy way out that has been taken by many people.

Why? The reason is that this God who seems so alien does indeed have something to do with human life. Without God life would have no further meaning: "They who are far from thee are lost; thou dost destroy all who wantonly forsake thee. But my chief good is to be near thee, O God; I have chosen thee, Lord God, to be my refuge" (Ps 73:27–28). Every human being looks for security in life, and the author of the Psalm has found a source of security so solid that he seems to be able to live tranquilly in the midst of life's turmoil: "Though heart and body fail, yet God is my possession for ever" (Ps 73:26).

God is the *foundation* and *future* of his life. Hence the psalmist possesses a rare brand of independence, solidity, freedom, and security that is the ideal yearned for by all people. Such a God really does have something to do with life.

True humanity, realism, and concern for everyday life pervade the Psalms. So it seems quite clear that *this* God, the God of the psalmist, is not a product of autosuggestion but rather a gratuitous reality benefiting humankind. Believing in this God makes a person more truly human, and great human qualities develop as a result of contact with God. Here we might enumerate a few of them:

1. The courage to live: "The Lord is the refuge of my life; of whom then should I go in dread? . . . If an army should encamp against me, my heart would feel no fear; if armed men should fall upon me, even then I should be undismayed" (Ps 27:1,3). It is the attitude of a mature person who knows what he wants. He has found his security in God.

2. A pervading sense of tranquillity: "Yet in my heart thou hast put more happiness than they enjoyed when there was corn and wine in plenty. Now I will lie down in peace, and sleep; for thou alone, O Lord, makest me live unafraid" (Ps 4:7–8).

3. Clear perception of what justice demands: "Who may go up the mountain of the Lord? And who may stand in his holy place? He who has clean hands and a pure heart, who has not set his mind on falsehood, and has not committed perjury. He shall receive a blessing from the Lord" (Ps 24:3–5). "O Lord, who may lodge in thy tabernacle? Who may dwell on thy holy mountain? The man of blameless life, who does what is right and speaks

the truth from his heart; who has no malice on his tongue, who never wrongs a friend and tells no tales against his neighbor; the man who shows his scorn for the worthless and honors all who fear the Lord; who swears to his own hurt and does not retract; who does not put his money out to usury and takes no bribe against an innocent man. He who does these things shall never be brought low" (Ps 15).

4. Courage to denounce the injustices committed by those in power: "Answer, you rulers: Are your judgments just? Do you decide impartially between man and man? Never! Your hearts devise all kinds of wickedness and survey the violence that you have done on earth" (Ps 58:1–2).

5. Clear awareness of God's justice, which makes one sure of the ultimate fate of the unjust: "The righteous shall rejoice that he has seen vengeance done, and shall wash his feet in the blood of the wicked, and men shall say, 'There is after all a reward for the righteous; after all, there is a God that judges on earth' " (Ps 58:10–11).

6. Rejection of any religion based solely on empty words or rites: "God's word to the wicked man is this: What right have you to recite my laws and make so free with the words of my covenant, you who hate correction and turn your back when I am speaking?" (Ps 50:16–17).

To know this God and share one's life with him is the most precious gift we can receive: "Thy true love is better than life" (Ps 63:3). Contact with this

God awakens us to the true values in our own life. We are brought back to life and new hope. From some deep source within us there wells up prayers of praise, thanksgiving, and supplication. We begin to understand the psalmist's feelings: "Whom have I in heaven but thee? And having thee, I desire nothing else on earth" (Ps 73:25). His real life is a continuing journey toward God: "But my chief good is to be near thee, O God; I have chosen thee, Lord God, to be my refuge" (Ps 73:28).

All the actions of such a person are a response to a summons in the inner depths of his being: "Come!' my heart has said, 'seek his face.' I will seek thy face, O Lord; do not hide it from me" (Ps 27:8–9). Listening to this inner voice will lead a person into the unpredictable and the unknown, for God is full of surprises. The immediate result of God's approach is obscurity, and only those who are willing to accept God into their lives wholeheartedly can make true progress. We must have firm confidence in this God, knowing that God's strength can get us through any crisis: "I wait for the Lord with all my soul, I hope for the fulfillment of his word" (Ps 130:5); "Well I know that I shall see the goodness of the Lord in the land of the living" (Ps 27:13).

When everything else fails, our only support is God. Though invisible, God is indeed with us: "I cry to thee, O Lord, and say, 'Thou art my refuge; thou art all I have in the land of the living' " (Ps 142:5). Treasuring this certainty, the faithful person keeps moving forward and waiting to hear the

friendly voice of God again some day. In the midst
of continuing crises, his attitude is: "I humbly follow thee with all my heart, and thy right hand is my
support" (Ps 63:8). This kind of person knows the
true law that governs existence: "Those who sow in
tears shall reap with songs of joy. A man may go out
weeping, carrying his bag of seed; but he will come
back with songs of joy, carrying home his sheaves"
(Ps 126:5–6).

If a person does not keep moving forward, he will
not perceive anything. He *must keep moving forward
with confidence and take the reins of history in his hands.*
Only then will he be able to put things in their
proper perspective, thanks to God's enlightenment. Only then will he be able to give up false
supports and fallacious certainties. Only then will
he be able to awaken to the authentic values in life,
to look to God as the *foundation* and *future* of his life.
To discover this foundation and future is to find
true peace: "O Lord, my heart is not proud, nor are
my eyes haughty. I do not busy myself with great
matters or things too marvellous for me. No, I sub-
mit myself, I account myself lowly, as a weaned
child clinging to its mother, O Israel, look for the
Lord now and evermore" (Ps 131).

That is what the Psalms tell us about God and
ourselves. They go to the core of the human problem. When they are well translated, they can be
taken over as an authentic expression of our own
experiences and hopes. They can then alert us to

certain features of life to which we do not pay sufficient attention.

The Raw Material for Prayer

Where are we to find the raw material for prayer? There is only one answer, and it can be put in one word. We find the raw material for prayer in *life*, in the life we are living. The affairs of life were like an alarm clock to the psalmist. Observing life, he was awakened to something else—or rather, to Someone else. Everything now reminded him of God: the happiness and sadness of life, nature with all its beauty and its dangers, history with all its twists and turns. Everything became transparent, revealing the God who was summoning and inspiring humankind. Almost without realizing it, he began to use the happenings of life as the raw material for conversation with God. Thus the Psalms welled up from *life with God*.

If we do not make this link with life, then all our talk about the Psalms will be in vain. It would be like buying a fine new television set and failing to plug it into the electric current. The television set might serve as a decorative piece of furniture, but it was not made for that purpose. The Psalms can serve to document the prayer life of people who lived long ago, but they were not meant to be historical archives. They were inspired to be recited; they were meant to awaken us to prayer here and now.